ENGLISH FOLK-SONG AND DANCE

ENGLISH FOLK-SONG
AND DANCE

BY
FRANK KIDSON
AND
MARY NEAL

Cambridge:
at the University Press
1915

CAMBRIDGE UNIVERSITY PRESS
Cambridge, New York, Melbourne, Madrid, Cape Town,
Singapore, São Paulo, Delhi, Tokyo, Mexico City

Cambridge University Press
The Edinburgh Building, Cambridge CB2 8RU, UK

Published in the United States of America by
Cambridge University Press, New York

www.cambridge.org
Information on this title: www.cambridge.org/9781107698253

© Cambridge University Press 1915

This publication is in copyright. Subject to statutory exception
and to the provisions of relevant collective licensing agreements,
no reproduction of any part may take place without the written
permission of Cambridge University Press.

First published 1915
First paperback edition 2011

A catalogue record for this publication is available from the British Library

ISBN 978-1-107-69825-3 Paperback

Cambridge University Press has no responsibility for the persistence or
accuracy of URLs for external or third-party internet websites referred to in
this publication, and does not guarantee that any content on such websites is,
or will remain, accurate or appropriate.

CONTENTS

ENGLISH FOLK-SONG

		PAGE
Introduction	. . . .	3
I. Definition	. . . .	9
II. The Origin of Folk-Song	. .	11
III. The Cante-Fable	. . .	15
IV. The Construction of Folk-Music	.	19
V. Changes that occur in Folk-Music	.	25
VI. The Quality of Folk-Song, and its Diffusion		36
VII. The Movement for collecting English Folk-Song	. . . .	40
VIII. The Noting of Folk-Music	. .	47
IX. The Different Classes of Folk-Song	.	52
X. The Narrative Ballad	. . .	53
XI. Love Songs and Mystic Songs	. .	57
XII. The Pastoral	. . . .	60
XIII. Drinking Songs and Humorous Songs	.	62
XIV. Highwayman and Poacher Songs	. .	64
XV. Soldier Songs	. . . .	66
XVI. Sea Songs	. . . .	67

		PAGE
XVII. PRESSGANG SONGS	. . . .	69
XVIII. HUNTING AND SPORTING SONGS	. .	70
XIX. SONGS OF LABOUR	. . . .	71
XX. TRADITIONAL CAROLS	. . .	74
XXI. CHILDREN'S SINGING-GAMES	. . .	77
XXII. THE BALLAD SHEET AND SONG GARLAND	.	78
BIBLIOGRAPHY	. . . .	86

ENGLISH FOLK-DANCE

INTRODUCTION	. . . .	97
I. THE MORRIS DANCE TO-DAY	. .	125
II. TUNES	. . . . .	130
III. MUSICAL INSTRUMENTS	. . .	132
IV. THE DRESS	. . . . .	136
V. EXTRA CHARACTERS	. . . .	141
VI. THE SWORD DANCE	. . . .	145
VII. THE FURRY DANCE	. . . .	150
VIII. THE COUNTRY DANCE	. . .	152
IX. THE PRESENT-DAY REVIVAL OF THE FOLK-DANCE	. . . . .	158
X. CONCLUSIONS	. . . .	167
BIBLIOGRAPHY	. . . .	173

LIST OF ILLUSTRATIONS

	FACING PAGE
MORRIS DANCERS AT BAMPTON-IN-THE-BUSH, OXON.	97
(By kind permission of *The Daily Chronicle*)	
ABINGDON DANCES, WHOSE TRADITION GOES BACK TO 1700	104
(From *The Espérance Morris Book*, Vol. I., by kind permission of Messrs J. Curwen & Son)	
MORRIS DANCERS IN THE TIME OF JAMES I.	120
MORRIS DANCE AND MUSIC	125
(From the *Orchesographie* of Thoinot-Arbeau, British Museum)	
WHIT-MONDAY AT BAMPTON-IN-THE-BUSH, OXON.	145
(By kind permission of *The Daily Chronicle*)	
THE LOCK; CHARACTERISTIC OF SWORD DANCES	148
(From *The Espérance Morris Book*, Vol. II., by kind permission of Messrs J. Curwen & Son)	

ENGLISH FOLK-SONG
BY FRANK KIDSON

NOTE

I am indebted to Miss Lucy E. Broadwood for permission to use a folk-tune of her collecting, and for many helpful suggestions.
F. K.

INTRODUCTION

WRITING two centuries ago, Joseph Addison tells us in the character of Mr Spectator:—

"When I travelled I took a particular delight in hearing the songs and fables that are come down from father to son, and are most in vogue among the common people of the countries through which I passed; for it is impossible that anything should be universally tasted and approved of by a multitude, though they are only the rabble of the nation, which hath not in it some peculiar aptness to please and gratify the mind of man" (*Spectator*, No. 70). He further says:—

"An ordinary song or ballad, that is the delight of the common people, cannot fail to please all such readers as are not unqualified for the entertainment by their affectation or ignorance."

It was not only the cultured Mr Addison who recognised the claims of the people's songs as expressive of sentiments that were worthy the consideration of the more learned, for quotation upon quotation could be given of examples where the refined and learned have found in the primitive song that which appealed in the highest degree.

The moderns need no excuse for the study of folk-song, and few will regard the consideration of people's-lore as an idle amusement.

The present essay is put forth with all diffidence as a very slight dissertation upon a complex subject, and it does not pretend to do more than enter into the fringe of it.

The younger of the present generation have seen the gradual speeding up of technique in composition and performance, but with this increased standard there has been a tendency to let fall certain very sacred and essential things that belong to musical art. In too many cases the composer has not quite justified the complexity of his composition; while glorying in the skill of his craftsmanship he has too frequently forgotten the primitive demand for art and beauty, apart from technical elaboration.

That type of simple melody that formerly pleased what we might regard as a less cultured age, holds no place in present-day composition or in the esteem of a certain class.

It is probable that this melodic starvation turned so many, who had not lost the feeling for simple tune, towards folk-music when this was dragged from obscurity and declared by competent musical

INTRODUCTION

judges to be worthy of consideration. Then people began to revel in its charm, and to feel that here was something that had been withheld from them, but which was good for their musical souls.

A simple air of eight or sixteen bars may not appear difficult to evolve, or even worth evolving at all, much less of record; but when the matter is further considered, we have to acknowledge that seemingly trivial melodies have wrought effects which have upset thrones and changed the fate of nations. Where they have not had this great political influence their histories show that they have rooted themselves deeply into the hearts of a people, and put into shade the finest compositions of great musicians. An undying vitality appears to be inherent in them, and this is shown by their general appeal throughout periods of thought and life totally unlike. Many examples prove this, and such an air as "Greensleeves" might be cited in this connexion.

One would suppose that nothing could be more apart in thought, action, and habit than the gallant of Elizabeth's reign and an English farm labourer of the present day. And yet the tune "Greensleeves" that pleased the sixteenth century culture is found the cherished possession of countrymen in the Midlands, who execute a rustic dance to a traditional survival of it. Further proof that it is one of those immortal tunes to which reference has been made is shown by the fact that it exists in various forms, and has had all kinds of songs fitted to it from its first recorded appearance in Shakespeare's time (who mentions it) down to the present day.

"Greensleeves" is probably an "art" tune and not strictly folk-music. Hence in its passage downwards it has gradually got stripped of some of its subtilty, as it has been chiefly passed onward by tradition. This change will be noted further on.

Other tunes that, coming from remote antiquity, still find a welcome with the people are, "John Anderson my Jo," and "Scots wha hae," while "Lillibulero," and "Boyne Water," though of lesser age, fall into the same category.

We have even taken to our hearts tunes of other nationalities, and perhaps have more French airs among our popular music than of any other country. As every student of national song knows, "We won't go home till morning" is but "Malbrook," the favourite of Marie Antoinette, who learned it from the peasant woman called in to nurse her first child. "Ah vous dirai je" is known as "Baa baa black sheep" in every nursery, while "In my cottage near a wood" is a literal translation from an old French song to its proper tune.

INTRODUCTION

Such of these, or of this class, as are not folk-tunes have the same spirit, and it is this indefinable quality that causes folk-music to be so tenacious of existence. If it be good enough it is almost impossible for it to die and be totally forgotten. A tune may lie dormant for half a century, but it rises again and has its period of renewed popularity. One might name many a music-hall air, over which the people have for a period gone half wild, that is merely a resuscitation of a tune that has pleased a former generation. Thus such airs pass through strata of widely differing thought and mode of life.

It is folk-music that appeals to the bed-rock temperament of the people. Artificial music can only do so to a culture, which may change its standards with a change of thought, and that which is the applauded of one generation becomes the despised of a succeeding one; musical history can furnish many such examples. These facts justify our appreciation of folk-music and elevate its study.

I. DEFINITION

THE word "folk-song" is so elastic in definition that it has been freely used to indicate types of song and melody that greatly differ from each other. The word conveys a different signification to different people, and writers have got sadly confused from this circumstance. Even the word "song" has not a fixed meaning, for it can imply both a lyric with its music, and the words of the lyric only.

"Folk-song," or "people's song," may be understood to imply, in its broadest sense, as *Volkslied* does to the German, a song and its music which is generally approved by the bulk of the people. Thus any current popular drawing-room song, or the latest music-hall production, would naturally hold this meaning, though it would not come into line with the other conceptions of folk-song, and probably not altogether satisfy the German ideal. Then, what may fitly be called "national" songs have a strong claim upon the word. "God save the King," "Home sweet Home," "Tom Bowling," "Heart of Oak," and countless others that form our national store of song and melody could under this meaning be called folk-songs, and this might come closer to the German idea of a *Volkslied*.

The type, however, which lies nearest the definition of folk-song, as understood by the modern expert, is a song born of the people and used by the people—practically exclusively used by them before being noted down by collectors and placed before a different class of singers. To pursue the subject further one might split straws over the word "people," but it may be generally accepted that "the people," in this instance, stands for a stratum of society where education of a literary kind is, in a greater or lesser degree, absent.

This last definition of folk-song, as "song and melody born of the people and used by the people as an expression of their emotions, and (as in the case of historical ballads) for lyrical narrative," is the one adopted in these pages and that generally recognised by the chief collectors and by the Folk-Song Society. In addition it may be mentioned that folk-song is practically almost always traditional, so far as its melody is concerned, and, like all traditional lore, subject to corruption and alteration. Also, that we have no definite knowledge of its original birth, and frequently but a very vague idea as to its period.

DEFINITION OF FOLK-SONG

It has been cleverly said that a proverb is the "wit of one and the wisdom of many." In a folk-song or folk-ballad we may accept a similar definition, to the effect that it is in the power of one person to put into tangible form a history, a legend, or a sentiment which is generally known to, or felt by, the community at large, but which few are able to put into definite shape. We may suppose that such effort from one individual may be either crude or polished; that matters little if the sentiment is a commonly felt one, for common usage will give it some degree of polish, or at any rate round off some of its corners.

II. THE ORIGIN OF FOLK-SONG

Every nation, both savage and civilized, has its folk-song, and this folk-song is a reflection of the current thought of the class among which it is popular. It is frequently a spontaneous production that invests in lyric form the commonly felt emotion or sentiment of the moment.

This type is more observable among savage tribes than among civilized nations. Folk-song is therefore not so permanent among the former as it is among the latter. So far as we can gather, though it is difficult to get at the truth of this matter, among primitive people the savage does not appear to retain his song-traditions, but invents new lyrics as occasion calls. For example, one is continually reading in books of travel of negroes, or natives of wild countries, chanting extemporary songs descriptive of things which have been the happenings of the day, and telling of the white man who has come among them, of the feast he has provided, of the dangers they have encountered during the journey, and so forth. The tunes of these songs appear to be chiefly monotonous chants, and the accompanying music of the rudest character, produced on tom-toms, horns, reed-flutes, or similar kinds of instruments. A very typical description of this class of folk-song, the like of which may be found in most books of travel, occurs in Day's *Music and Musical Instruments of Southern India and the Deccan.* The author says:—

"The ordinary folk-songs of the country are called "Lavanis," and will be familiar to every one who has heard the coolies sing as they do their work, the women nursing their children, the bullock-drivers and dooley-bearers, or Sepoys on the march. The airs are usually very monotonous, the words, if not impromptu, are a sort of history, or ballad in praise of some warrior, or

THE ORIGIN OF FOLK-SONG

'burra-sahib.' Some have a kind of chorus, each in turn singing an improvised verse."

This type appears to be the origin of a nation's folk-song.

It is a sign of a country's civilization when it begins to keep records, either by tradition or more fixed methods, and it is a theory (which may be probably accepted as correct) that chronicles were first chanted in ballad form and thus more easily passed downward in remembrance. This may be accepted as the origin of the folk-ballad. Its music has originated by the same natural instinct that produces language.

Much has been said of the communal origin of folk-song and folk-music, but it is somewhat difficult fully to realise what is meant by such a term in relation to these matters.

Those who hold this theory appear to assert that a folk-song with its music has had a primal formation at some early and indefinite time, and that this germ, thrown upon the world, has been fashioned and changed by numberless brains according to the popular demand, and has only met with general acceptance when it has fulfilled the requirements that the populace have demanded. This change is called its "evolution," and it is sometimes claimed that this evolution still goes on where folk-songs are yet sung; this means that the folk-song is virtually in a state of fluidity.

Such, briefly, appears to be the idea of those who hold the evolutionary, or communal, theory of folk-song origin. It cannot be denied that there is an obvious truth in such a contention, but before it can be generally accepted surely there must be much modification. It cannot be altogether decided that the original germ is absolutely different from the folk-song as found existing to-day, but that both folk-song and folk-music are subject to change also cannot be disputed. The parlour game "Gossip," in which A whispers a short narrative to B, who in turn whispers it to C, the narrative passing finally to Z, has been used as an illustration of the variations that folk-song undergoes. In the game, the tale originally put forth by A is generally found to be much unlike that received by Z. Folk-song in some degree suffers such change by conscious or unconscious alteration. Unconscious alteration we can easily understand; that is merely the result of imperfect remembrance. Conscious alteration may be the effect, in vocal rendering, of a difficulty in individual singers of attaining certain intervals, or from choice. Alteration in instrumental rendering of folk-music is chiefly due to lack of skill in the performer on a particular instrument. Thus, what may be diffi-

THE ORIGIN OF FOLK-SONG

cult to render on a flute may be easy on a fiddle; hence we can conceive an alteration may be purposely made for facility of performance. This is decidedly not evolution, nor communal origin.

III. THE CANTE-FABLE

THE existence of the "Cante-fable" has furnished another theory of folk-song origin. The Cante-fable is a traditional prose narrative having rhymed passages incorporated with the tale. These rhymes are generally short verses, or couplets, which recur at dramatic points of the story. They were probably sung to tunes, but present-day remembrance has failed to preserve more than a few specimens, and the verse, or couplet, is now generally recited.

It has been asserted that the Cante-fable is a sort of germ from which both ballad and prose narrative have evolved. Mr Jacobs, in *English Fairy Tales*, says—"The Cante-fable is probably the protoplasm out of which both ballad and folk-tale have been differentiated; the ballad by omitting the narrative prose, and the folk-tale by expanding it."

Mr Cecil J. Sharp, in *English Folk-song: Some*

Conclusions, p. 6, tells of having noted a version of the ballad "Lord Thomas and Fair Eleanor"—"in which the whole of the story was sung, with the exception of three lines, which the singer assured me should be spoken. This was clearly a case of a Cante-fable that had very nearly, but not quite, passed into the form of a ballad, thus corroborating Mr Jacobs' theory."

The present writer is sorry to differ from Mr Jacobs as well as from Mr Sharp in this matter, but he does not think that facts quite justify the conclusion. He can but look upon the speaking of the three lines of the "Fair Eleanor" ballad, instead of singing them, as merely an individual eccentricity that has no value as pointing to a nearly completed evolution. Their theory indicates, to put it crudely, that the Cante-fable is in the condition of a tadpole which by and by will have its fins and tail turned into legs, will forsake its original element, and hop about a meadow, instead of being entirely confined to pond water.

An examination of existing Cante-fables will certainly reveal the fact that the fragments of verse are used either as a literary ornament, or to force some particular dramatic situation home to the hearer. Also, it must be noticed that the rhyme passages are not merely fragmentary parts

THE CANTE-FABLE

of a prose narrative which is gradually turning wholly into rhyme, but most frequently consist of a repeated verse, or couplet, that occurs at parts of the story, which could not be so effectively told in prose.

The commonly known story of "Orange," versions of which, all having the same rhyme passages, are to be found in English, German, and other folk-tales is a good example. With little variation the story tells of a stepmother who kills her husband's child, makes the body into a pie, to be eaten by the father, and buries the bones in the cellar. First one member of the family goes into this place and hears the voice of the murdered child sing,—

> "My mother did kill me and put me in pies,
> My father did eat me and say I was nice;
> My two little sisters came picking my bones,
> And buried me under cold marble stones."

Then other members of the family go to the cellar and in turn hear the same voice repeating the rhyme (see *Folk-Song Journal*, vol. ii., p. 295, for a version of the tale and a tune sung to the above words learned from Liverpool children).

Another Cante-fable, surely a genuine one, is given by Charles Dickens in "Nurses' Stories" in *The Uncommercial Traveller*.

In this case the rhyme—
> "A lemon has pips,
> A yard has ships,
> And I'll have Chips!"

is brought out with vivid effect by the narrator at intervals and with terror-striking force due to its expected recurrence, just as in the case of the story of "Orange." As Dickens puts it—"I don't know why, but the fact of the Devil expressing himself in rhyme was peculiarly trying to me." And again—"For this refrain I had waited since its last appearance with inexpressible horror, which now culminated." And—"The invariable effect of this alarming tautology on the part of the Evil Spirit was to deprive me of my senses."

There can be but little doubt that this Cante-fable is a real nurse's story, remembered by the great author from his childhood, and Dickens so well describes the feeling of terror that the rhyme inspires in the childish listener, that we cannot but grant that the original makers of Cante-fable were quite alive to the dramatic force such recurring rhymes possess.

Other examples of the Cante-fable are to be found in Chambers' *Popular Rhymes of Scotland* and elsewhere. All, however, point to the verse being used as an ornamental and dramatic addition to the story, and certainly not as indicating a transitionary stage between a rhyming and a prose narrative.

The question of a Cante-fable origin of the folk-ballad is here somewhat fully dealt with, as it is a sufficiently romantic theory to lead people, who have not fully considered all the points involved, to accept it on trust.

IV. THE CONSTRUCTION OF FOLK-MUSIC

It will be quite evident to the average hearer that much folk-music is built upon scales different from those that form the foundation of the ordinary modern tune. This fact is accounted for by the circumstance that a large percentage of folk-melodies are "modal"; *i.e.* constructed upon the so-called "ecclesiastical modes" which, whether adopted from the Greek musical system or not, had Greek nomenclature, and were employed in the early church services.

The ecclesiastical scales may be realised by playing an octave scale on the white keys of the piano only. Thus—C to C is Ionian, D to D Dorian, E to E Phrygian, F to F Lydian (rarely used), G to G Mixolydian, A to A Æolian, and B to B Locrian (practically unused).

Progress in harmony and polyphony gradually revealed the cramping effect of many modal intervals, and already by the beginning of the seventeenth century our modern major and minor scales (the first, however, corresponding to the Ionian mode in structure) had supplanted the rest, so far as trained musicians were concerned. Not so with the folk-tune maker; he was conservative enough to preserve that which had become obsolete elsewhere. We find a large proportion of folk-airs are in the Dorian, Mixolydian, and Æolian modes, with much fewer in the Phrygian.

When folk-music began to be first studied scientifically a theory was held that because of its modal character it was necessarily a reflex of ecclesiastical music, and that secular melodies were either church chants set to songs, or in some other way derived from them. It is known that many of the early clerics established schools for the teaching of music, with intent to enrich the services. But while this theory is temptingly plausible, yet it is incapable of proof, and a reverse one might, with equal reason, be held to maintain that the church took its music directly from the people, or at any rate adapted its form from that mostly popular.

It has also been asserted that the modal character of folk-music is a clear proof of great age. It is certainly more than likely that most of the modal tunes that are found are of considerable antiquity, but it is scarcely safe to conclude that all are so. How old any particular folk-tune may be is a problem incapable of solution, and all attempts to fix its age and period can be but, at best, mere guesswork.

We may grant that folk-music has been handed down traditionally by many generations of singers, but if it has pleased these different generations we must also admit that any new composition of folk-music, to please the people, must conform to their common demand.

Folk-music seems to have held its own traditional ideals longer and more closely than music composed for that class which has so persistently ignored it. The cultured musician is always, consciously or unconsciously, influenced by the music of his day, and as a consequence adheres to its idioms, or is genius enough to found a school of his own. His music too is far more elaborate than that produced by the rustic, or untaught musician. It has harmony, and many more points of evidence that enable us definitely to fix its period of composition.

The composer of folk-music may be compared,

in a sense, to the Indian, or Chinese art-worker who repeats the class of patterns that has come down to him from time immemorial. When European influence was brought to bear on his work his patterns became debased, lost their original beauty, and gained nothing from the new source of inspiration.

There is no space in this small manual to enter into a disquisition on the Modes. The reader is referred to such a work as the new edition of Grove's *Dictionary of Music and Musicians* (vol. iii., p. 222), to Carl Engel's *Study of National Music*, and to a most valuable contribution to the subject by Miss A. G. Gilchrist, "Note on the Modal System of Gaelic Tunes," in the *Journal of the Folk-Song Society*, vol. iv., No. 16.

The following are given as examples of modal folk-tunes, in the modes most frequently found:—

ONE MOONLIGHT NIGHT

DORIAN *Sung in a " Cante-Fable "*

One moonlight night, as I sat high, I looked for one, but two came by; The boughs did bend, the leaves did shake, To see the hole the fox did make.

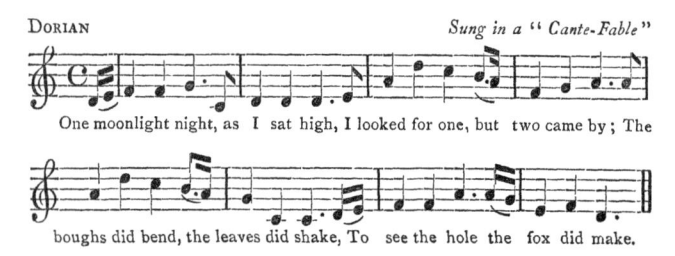

FOLK-TUNES 23

THE BONNY LABOURING BOY

Noted by Miss L. E. Broadwood   *Sung by Mr Lough, Surrey*

MIXOLYDIAN

As I roved out one eve-ning, being in the blooming spring,

I heard a love-ly dam-sel fair most grie-vously did sing, Say-ing

"Cru-el were my pa-rents that did me so an-noy. They

did not let me mar-ry with my bon-ny la-b'ring boy.

CHRISTMAS CAROL AS SUNG IN NORTH YORKSHIRE

ÆOLIAN MODE

God rest you merry, merry gentle-men, Let nothing you dis-may, Re-

member Christ our Saviour was born on Christmas day, To

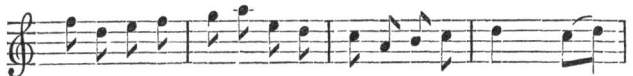

save our souls from Satan's pow'r that long had gone a-stray, Oh, *tid - ings of com - fort and joy, and joy, and joy, Oh, tid - ings of com - fort and joy, and joy.*

In addition to modal tunes we have a certain number of folk-airs built upon a "gapped," or limited, scale of five notes instead of the usual seven. This "pentatonic" scale, which appears to be very characteristic of the primitive music of all nations, was formerly held as an infallible sign of a Scottish origin, and the old recipe to produce a Scottish air was—"stick to the black keys of the piano." It is quite true that a large number of Scottish melodies have the characteristics of the pentatonic scale, but so also have the Irish tunes, and there are a lesser number that may claim to be English.

Much nonsense has been written to account for the existence of the pentatonic scale, the general conclusion arrived at being that it arose from the use of an imperfect instrument that could only produce five tones. Whatever the instrument so limited may have been, it was neither the primitive flute (like the tin whistle) of six vents, which is sufficient to produce well over an octave, nor was it the human voice. The universal use of the five-

FOLK-MUSIC

note scale among many nations wide apart has never been satisfactorily explained. The following is an Irish pentatonic traditional air.

THE SHAMROCK SHORE
PENTATONIC

V. CHANGES THAT OCCUR IN FOLK-MUSIC

THAT all traditional lore is subject to change is of course a well-recognised fact, and this change is so uncertain in its effects, and so erratic in its selection that no law appears to govern it. In ballads or prose narratives that exist only by verbal transmission we may expect the dropping of obsolete words and phrases, and this usually occurs; though sometimes corruptions of such remain and are meaningless to those who repeat them.

For instance, in a certain singing-game, children of a particular district were accustomed to say—

"She knocked at the door and picked up a pin."
It is quite obvious that the original stood—

"She knocked at the door and tirled at the pin." The "tirling pin" having completely gone out of usage, and even out of popular remembrance, in the limited area where it formerly served the purpose of attracting the attention of the householder, the phrase would have no meaning to the modern child; hence the change into something more comprehensible.

There is considerable analogy in the above to the change that takes place in folk-music. But as musical phrases do not, at any rate in folk-music, become so obsolete as words, the variation is less considerable and is probably due to different causes. These are chiefly wilful alteration for particular reasons, and unconscious change due to lapse of memory, or imperfect hearing. We may usefully consider two or three examples of these kinds of alterations. The tune "Greensleeves" is a very characteristic instance. The first record of the song is at the date 1580, when the ballad was entered at Stationers' Hall. It is evident that

CHANGES IN FOLK-MUSIC 27

both words and tune became immediately popular, and from that time to our own day it has always retained considerable favour, for it was one of those stock tunes used for ephemeral political ditties, and for the scraps of verse that were employed in the early ballad operas. It is easy to trace, from the eighteenth century printed copies, how the tendency has been to eliminate complex passages, and generally to simplify, while retaining the essential features of the tune. Probably this is its pure sixteenth century form—

GREENSLEEVES

(*Earliest form*) 16th Century

28 ENGLISH FOLK-SONG

It is rather a shock to find that the beautiful air has by careless transmission or wilful change got so degraded as finally to appear in a manuscript book of fiddle airs dated 1838, thus,—

GREENSLEEVES

From a Manuscript Book, dated 1838

Other copies which have deplorably lost much of the purity of the original are to be seen in D'Urfey's *Wit and Mirth*, *The Beggar's Opera* and other early eighteenth century publications. This is from an edition of *The Dancing Master*, dated 1716:

GREENSLEEVES AND YELLOW LACE

Printed 1716

We may trace a curious corruption in the tune as found in traditional usage in Ireland nearly eighty years ago. Thomas Moore employed this traditional version for his song, "Oh, could we do with this world of ours," and published it united to his verses in his *Irish Melodies*, the tenth number dated 1834. He gives the tune the name of "The Basket of Oysters." The real tune which went by this title, otherwise known as "Paddy the Weaver," is to be seen in Aird's *Selection of Scotch, English, Irish and Foreign Airs*, vol. iii., Glasgow [1788], and elsewhere. It will be noticed that Moore's tune is "Greensleeves," to which is joined a part of "Paddy the Weaver." It is a notable example of the manner in which traditional tunes suffer change from imperfect remembrances or other causes.

THE BASKET OF OYSTERS

Greensleeves, Irish Version, 1834

30 ENGLISH FOLK-SONG

A BASKET OF OYSTERS, or PADDY THE WEAVER

From Aird's "Selection," 1788

Although "Greensleeves" is probably not a folk-tune, yet in some cases folk-tunes are apt to suffer a like degradation in character, although it must be clearly stated that tradition frequently holds them together in a wonderfully perfect manner.

In this latter case we may rank "Joan's

CHANGES IN FOLK-MUSIC

placket is torn," which survives in the modern "Cock o' the North," with "Greensleeves," and their histories are well worth recalling.

We may pass over the tradition that "Joan's placket" was played at the execution of Mary Queen of Scots. The structure of the tune shows it to have been originally a trumpet tune, and strangely enough throughout the whole course of its existence it seems to have been used in defiance or ridicule. Mr Pepys tells us that when the English sailors left the deserted "Royal Charles" in the Medway in 1667, a Dutch trumpeter sounded the tune from the deck of the captured ship. After this period political lampoons were adapted to the melody. It is difficult to find out when the tune was first named "The Cock o' the North," or when, under that title, it was adopted as a British army tune, but there is a striking instance of its use during the siege of Lucknow in the Mutiny of 1857. It was the practice to signal by flag and bugle call from the City to the Residency, both in a state of siege. On one occasion a drummer boy, named Ross, after the signalling was over again climbed to the high dome from which it was conducted, and in spite of the Sepoy rifles sounded "The Cock o' the North" as a defiance. We all know the story of the wounded piper, shot in the ankle during the rush at Dargai, crouching behind a rock and still sounding the pipe tune the "Cock o' the North" that had inspired the onslaught. How little the traditional "Cock o' the North" differs from "Joan's Placket" the reader will be able to see from the following copies:—

JOAN'S PLACKET IS TORN

17th Century

THE COCK O' THE NORTH

20th Century

CHANGES IN FOLK-MUSIC

Many other examples of traditional cohesion as regards folk-tunes might be cited did space permit.

The tune "A sailor loved a farmer's daughter," given in Edward Bunting's *Ancient Music of Ireland*, 1840, has recently been noted from a farm labourer by Mrs Stanton of Armscott, Warwickshire, in a form practically identical with the printed version, though it is quite evident that the tune noted in Warwickshire has had a source independent of Bunting's. Every collector could point to such instances from his own experience.

Another fact forces itself into notice. A tune may develop by traditional passage, or by wilful alteration, into several forms, and thus we get airs having points of similarity but also points of difference. In some cases the likeness may be so close that the different tunes are classed as "variants."

It must be realised that a folk-song singer is under no bond to sing an air strictly as he has received it. Fortunately, in many cases, as shown above, he does, and religiously adheres to the melody as far as his memory, or skill, will permit. There are, however, difficult tunes to remember as well as easy ones, and this fact has considerable bearing on the question.

The reason why we find well-known folk-songs adapted to different airs is somewhat obvious, and the following explanation may be I think accepted. Where a singer reads a folk-song from a ballad sheet and does not know its particular tune, it is easy to believe that he uses one with which he is already familiar, or adapts one, or even composes an air from the stock musical phrases that he knows in other melodies. Thus we find folk-songs sung to many different airs, and this is not evolution.

It may be noticed that in the lesser marked tunes, or rather less original airs, stock musical phrases are in use just as the stock phrases of the ballad-maker are employed by him over and over again. The folk-song singer looks for and welcomes these passages. They are conventional and are the most acceptable. Just as a child gives a better welcome to a story beginning "Once upon a time" than to a less hackneyed manner of opening, and as the folk-singer demands that every girl shall be "a fair damsel," that the incident of the song shall happen "As I was a-walking one morning in May," and that his mode of address shall be "I stepped up boldly to her," or the like, so there are certain inevitable musical phrases in folk-music that one meets with in a particular type of melody.

Waggish musicians are sometimes guilty of inventing "a folk-melody" for the purpose of

CHANGES IN FOLK-MUSIC

deceiving and laughing at collectors. The collector, recognising the phrases he knows so well, may accept the tune as genuine. He is not wrong or ignorant in this; the musician has got possession of the material and spirit of folk-music, and then deception is easy. A man may have a Johnsonian method of diction without having the wit or learning of the great lexicographer, and might even pass off a short speech as a genuine one of the Doctor's.

These stock phrases are of course freely used in folk-music, and it is quite easy for a singer of folk-song legitimately to make an air for a ballad whose proper tune he may not know. This is another way in which variation of tunes occurs, and such results are frequently very puzzling to the expert. The singer may have remembered a passage of a melody and to this he has fitted other phrases that he is also familiar with. He is probably not conscious of the composite tune he is making,—he may even think that he is singing the correct tune.

VI. THE QUALITY OF FOLK-SONG, AND ITS DIFFUSION

THE strongest and most valuable feature of folk-song is its earnestness and good faith. Though the quality of earnestness is indefinable it is the soul of art work, and its presence is ever felt.

A folk-song may be very doggerel in verse, its subject trite and trivial, yet it possesses that subtle character that has the appeal and lasting power only belonging to sincerity. The maker of a folk-song did not produce his work for professional reasons; he sang because he must, and sometimes he was very ill-fitted for the task. Yet the work, being done in good faith, has not only the power of appeal to the class for which it was made, but also to a higher culture. Work of greater cleverness if it lack this great asset of earnestness cannot do more than please a particular cult for the moment.

As with folk-music and folk-song, so with the original folk-song singer. In general he does not sing anything that is not fully in accord with his own sentiments, and this is really why folk-song not only keeps in favour with him, but also why it maintains its integrity in tradition. It is seldom, except for the reasons I have before given, that a

DIFFUSION OF FOLK-SONG 37

folk-song singer wilfully alters his song. As I have said, he may, and indeed frequently does, make unconscious changes, but he has a respect for the songs handed down to him.

On the other hand a singer will without scruple rob another district of its right in a folk-song. What in one district is "Scarbro' Fair" becomes "Whittingham Fair," and "Birmingham Fair" becomes "Brocklesby Fair," according to the places where the songs are current. Otherwise the song sustains no material change, and each set of singers will declare their own version is the true one.

The drawing-room vocalist has not the same constancy to his songs as the folk-song singer, nor have his songs the same stability. When the stout respectable father of a family proclaims his passion for a fascinating nymph, and entreats her to fly with him, his wife smiles approval and silently applauds his efforts. When a feeble-looking young man voices sentiments of a bloodthirsty or gruesome character nobody is expected to believe him. In fact he is not in earnest, and in neither of the two cases I have supposed do the singers voice their general sentiments. On the other hand, the folk-song singer really *does* feel the sentiments he sings. If he likes fox-hunting, he sings a fox-hunting song, and is in perfect agreement with the ditty that proclaims foxhunting a noble sport. And the song represents his feelings when he sings of the joys of farming, or of good liquor, or any other subject that appeals to him as a man, including love. When a young girl or even an old lady sings—

> "Oh, my very heart is breaking
> All for the love of him,"

we may be quite sure that this puts into song some sentiments that either hold possession of the soul or recalls certain sacred memories.

Such songs as voice commonly felt sentiments are quickly diffused over the countryside, and they are to be found very widely spread. Where songs deal with the usages of a district, which, from some cause or another, do not obtain elsewhere, they are less likely to travel. For example, we find few harvest home songs current in the north of England, and not so many that deal with the joys of farming. In the south-west, where there are large tracts of agricultural land, and more organised merry-makings at the close of the harvest, or at sheep-shearing, there are plenty of songs which proclaim that the life of a farmer, or a ploughman, is all that can be desired.

In the North, where there is more grazing land, and the harvest is harder to wring from the soil,

DIFFUSION OF FOLK-SONG 39

this type of song scarcely exists. The fact is therefore again forced upon us that the folk-song singer, or maker, deals with things with which he is most familiar. Except for these limitations it is unsafe to class a folk-song as " Yorkshire," " Devonshire," or otherwise fix it to a particular county.

There are, of course, a very small number of folk-songs that obviously belong to certain districts, but because a song is sung or noted in one county we cannot claim that such county is the place of its origin. Before folk-song collecting was so general as at present it was frequently customary to fall into this error, but as collectors and their published " finds " have increased in number, it has become apparent that folk-songs have been very widespread.

For some reason a song may linger longer in one place than another. Such a one may be compared to the snow which may have completely covered a hill-side, but ultimately melting leaves its remnants only in the sheltered nooks, to disappear last of all.

In a similar way we may find that a dialect word which might be hastily assumed to belong strictly to, say, Yorkshire, is used in another part of the country—quite remote, and is generally considered to be a local word. Instances of such might be given, and we may speculate as to how the word, or the song has got there, whether by travel, or whether, like the snowdrift, by survival.

VII. THE MOVEMENT FOR COLLECTING ENGLISH FOLK-SONG

It remains now to consider what has been done towards the noting of traditional songs and their airs. Little attention was paid to the songs sung by country singers prior to the first half of the nineteenth century. In England, the first step toward the recognition of country folk-song was made by the Rev. John Broadwood, squire of Lyne, on the Sussex and Surrey border. In 1843 he published (modestly keeping his name from the title page) a collection of sixteen songs which were harmonised by a country organist. The title of the Rev. John Broadwood's book is lengthy, but so curious and explanatory that I reproduce it. The work itself is of extraordinary rarity.

" Old English Songs, as now sung by the peasantry of the weald of Surrey and Sussex, and collected by one who has learnt them by hearing them sung every Christmas from early childhood

FOLK-SONG COLLECTING

by the country people who go about to the neighbouring houses, singing, or 'wassailing,' as it is called, at that season. The airs are set to music exactly as they are now sung, to rescue them from oblivion, and to afford a specimen of genuine old English Melody, and the words are given in their original rough state with an occasional slight alteration to render the sense intelligible. Harmonised for the collector, in 1843, by G. A. Dusart, organist to the Chapel of Ease at Worthing. London, Published for the Collector by Balls & Co., 408 Oxford St. for private circulation (folio, pp. 32)."

It was about this time that William Chappell was bringing into notice the fine store of English melodies, which were then quite unknown save to a few musical antiquaries. He had already published a couple of volumes of airs, but in 1856 he commenced the issue of his *Popular Music of the Olden Time*, and among the tunes there printed he included a small number of traditional melodies which he had taken down chiefly in the South of England. Many of these have won their way into the hearts of lovers of our national music, and it seems a pity that they are omitted from the new edition of Chappell's work. For a long time after Chappell's publication little attention was paid to the folk-songs of our own country, though many

German songs that claimed to be people's song obtained considerable favour with us. About 1878 a revival of interest in the Northumbrian small pipes caused a search to be made for pipe tunes, and Mr John Stokoe, of South Shields, was an active worker in the field. Commencing in December 1878 he contributed to the *Newcastle Courant* a series of pipe and fiddle tunes once popular among Northumbrian pipers. They were chiefly taken from manuscript collections, but while the airs were, in many cases, merely transcripts from books of printed tunes for the violin or flute, published in England and Scotland during the eighteenth and early nineteenth centuries, there remained a number of traditional melodies of purely Northumbrian usage.

In 1882, under the auspices of the Society of Antiquaries, Newcastle-on-Tyne, Mr Stokoe, in collaboration with Dr Collingwood Bruce, published a volume entitled *Northumbrian Minstrelsy*, and here the *Courant* tunes were republished with other material. The work has the fault of including as fresh material much of what had already been printed in early dance collections and elsewhere, but having small claim to be considered as of Northumbrian origin.

A book of traditional nursery rhymes, chiefly from a Northumbrian source, had already been

FOLK-SONG COLLECTING 43

issued (in 1877) by Miss M. A. Mason. In 1888 a small illustrated booklet, *The Besom Maker and other Country Folk-Songs*, containing nine songs, was issued by Mr Heywood Sumner.

It was about this period that a wave of sympathy impelled several persons to turn their attention to the consideration of the songs sung by rustics and other persons who remembered the songs sung by their parents or elders. Most persons were under the impression that these country songs were merely remembrances from printed sources, and that practically little, or nothing, existed purely traditionary.

A little study of the question, however, soon convinced Miss Lucy E. Broadwood, Dr William Alexander Barrett, the Rev. Sabine Baring-Gould, and the present writer to the contrary.

Miss Broadwood, then living at Lyne in Sussex, found an unworked mine of great richness among the country people of her district. The late Dr Barrett had already gathered much, chiefly in the South of England, while a chance suggestion at a dinner-table caused Mr Baring-Gould to turn his attention to the collecting of the song current in Devonshire and Cornwall. Mr Baring-Gould absolutely revelled in this work, and his wild journeys over Dartmoor, with periods of settling down for a time at village inns, brought him in a plentiful harvest of charming songs and delightful melody. In this task he was associated with the Rev. H. Fleetwood Sheppard and Mr F. W. Bussell. The work of these collectors saw publication in *Songs of the West*, the first part of which was issued about 1889, and the fourth and last part in 1891.

Another work of Mr Baring-Gould's, in conjunction with the late Mr Sheppard, is a *Garland of Country Songs*, 1895. This is some portion of the material left over from *Songs of the West*; both were published by Methuen. A re-issue of *Songs of the West* with additions appeared in 1905.

A small part of Miss Broadwood's work was incorporated in *English County Songs*, which she edited in collaboration with Mr J. A. Fuller Maitland in 1893. The great popularity of this work is justified by its excellence. A further selection appeared in *English Traditional Songs and Carols* (Boosey, 1908).

Dr Wm. Alex. Barrett, in February 1891, a few months prior to his death, issued, through Novello & Co., *English Folk-Songs*, a most interesting collection of fifty-four songs, some of which, however, are to be found in print in earlier publications.

In the spring of 1891 the present writer issued

THE FOLK-SONG SOCIETY 45

the result of his collecting under the title *Traditional Tunes, a collection of ballad airs chiefly obtained in Yorkshire and the South of Scotland, by Frank Kidson*.

After these publications no further work on English folk-song appeared before the formation of the Folk-Song Society. This society, the most important factor in calling attention to the existence of unnoted folk-song, owed its existence to three or four enthusiasts in the cause who saw the utility of such a thing. At first it was projected as a branch of the Folk-Lore Society, but, finally, it was thought advisable that it should stand alone. The Folk-Song Society was duly formed on June 16th, 1898. The first president was the late Lord Herschell; the vice-presidents the late Sir John Stainer, Sir Alexander Mackenzie, Sir Hubert Parry, Professor (now Sir Charles) Stanford, and the committee as follows—Mrs Frederick Beer, Miss Lucy E. Broadwood, Sir Ernest Clarke, Mr W. H. Gill, Mrs (now Lady) Gomme, Messrs A. P. Graves, (the late) E. F. Jacques, Frank Kidson, J. A. Fuller Maitland, J. P. Rogers, W. Barclay Squire, and Dr Todhunter. The late Mrs Kate Lee acted as Hon. Secretary and Mr A. Kalisch as Hon. Treasurer, both being on the committee.

In the first year 110 members joined; at the

present time there are probably more than three times that number. In 1904 Miss Lucy E. Broadwood became Hon. Secretary, and the useful work of the society advanced by leaps and bounds. Mrs Walter Ford, and Mr Frederick Keel, the present secretary, followed Miss Broadwood.

The " Journals " of the Society, which by January 1914 had reached eighteen issues, are of the utmost importance in the study of folk-song. They contain material gathered by members of the Society in different parts of the United Kingdom. The original members of the Council of the Folk-Song Society who have died or retired have been replaced by musicians and collectors equally enthusiastic, and such additional names as Dr Vaughan Williams, Mr Percy Grainger, Mr Clive Carey, and Mr Cecil J. Sharp bear witness to the excellent hands in which the Society is held.

It would be invidious to name the individual members who have supplied matter to the Journals of the Folk-Song Society, but besides the above named, Miss A. G. Gilchrist, the late Dr Gardiner, the late H. E. D. Hammond, Mrs Leather, Miss Tolmie (with her Gaelic songs), and Mr W. P. Merrick have all contributed largely and well. Miss Gilchrist has written with great knowledge on the construction of folk-tunes, and has supplied other notes of much value.

THE FOLK-SONG SOCIETY 47

English folk-song and folk-music has been utilised in several compositions by Dr Vaughan Williams, Mr H. Balfour Gardiner, Mr Rutland Boughton, and Mr Percy Grainger.

The part that Mr Cecil Sharp has taken in the advancement of folk-song is well known. He has collected extensively, chiefly in Somerset, and his vigorous methods of bringing the subject before the public have caused "folk-song" to become a household word wherever the English language is spoken.

VIII. THE NOTING OF FOLK-MUSIC

WHEN the songs and the ballads of the people began to be recognised as belonging, more or less, to literature, the editors of collections deemed it was essential that their crudities of style, rhyme, and diction should be amended, and that the whole should undergo a polishing process before being launched to the public.

Bishop Percy, of course, naturally occurs to one's mind in this connection, and we must grant that in the classic age when he issued his three volumes (1765) there was reason on his side, and he had some justification for the trimming he did

—the world was not yet ripe for the folk-ballad collector.

There is much reason to suspect the later editors of ballad lore did as much as Percy in the work of polishing, and even went beyond him by pure fabrication. No excuse for such work as this nowadays exists. People are quite prepared to accept fragments of traditional ballads or songs precisely in the state they are sung or recited.

In a much lesser degree the same kind of thing held as regards certain earlier collectors of folk-music. This attitude was not one of deceit, but rather of ignorance. The modal influence on folk-music was not understood. As a consequence intervals were altered to conform to the harmony of another scale. As folk-music began to be better realised more scientific knowledge was brought to bear on the subject, and every nerve strained to obtain accuracy of notation.

The phonograph at once suggested itself as a ready and accurate instrument for the work of noting traditional melody, and many collectors employ it for this purpose. There is, however, a section of workers in folk-song who rather mistrust its claim to give the best results. The motive that inspires the use of the phonograph is praiseworthy in the extreme, but those opposed to its use suggest that these results are sometimes

THE NOTING OF FOLK-MUSIC 49

not very satisfactory where transcriptions taken directly from phonograph records have been published. They are generally complex and confusing, and for examples of the excessively elaborate rhythms and shifting tonality from phonographic records, the reader is invited to refer to some particular Journals of the Folk-Song Society. The transcriber should certainly bear in mind that mixed rhythms (2-4 time changing to 6-8, 7-8, 4-4, 5-8, and so forth in one short air) can hardly belong to the original structure of the tune, but rather to the method of singing it. If the performance of any great singer were phonographed, and its actual note-value faithfully transcribed, this would scarcely be considered a fair way of treating it. It would show a complexity of rhythms of which both the singer and the audience would be quite unaware. The composer would most certainly repudiate such a notation, though he might be quite satisfied with the singer's treatment of the piece. He would claim that the most legitimate method would be to indicate time-deviations by the ordinary accepted marks of expression.

The difficulty of noting melodies from the ordinary possessor of folk-song is very great, and varies with every singer. Some are a delight to listen to, others, though it is quite evident that they possess songs and melodies of the highest interest, produce an opposite effect on the listener. A phonographic record from one would be a joy, from the other a painful experience.

Practically every singer of original folk-song is an amateur, and this by no means lessens the beauty of his singing; in many cases, though, it offers much disadvantage to the one who notes his tunes. Unconsciously the vocalist sings the air frequently with more or less slight difference, and is sometimes not quite true to his note or key. Any mechanical contrivance for noting his song reproduces these inaccuracies, and, what is still more to the point, eight folk-singers out of ten asked to sing into that strange funnel above a moving cylinder will be nervous and not sing their best, either in time or tune. A sturdy young farmer, perhaps, who knows all about the gramophone, may come out of the ordeal with flying colours, and his strong masculine voice be reproduced with good effect, but not so a feeble old lady whose songs can only be obtained by careful tact and sympathetic manner, nor can such be noted otherwise than by getting constant repetitions and making selections from her differing renderings.

It is the business of the folk-song collector not to make a hard and fast record of one rendering of a folk-tune, with all its accidental inaccuracies,

THE NOTING OF FOLK-MUSIC

but to obtain what the singer obviously means. Where possible, the best rendering should be given in its full integrity, and any emendation stated as such, with reasons given for the alteration. It is too much to expect that every folk-song singer should be a paragon of faithful accuracy. In many cases, as before observed, he sings his tune with some difference on occasions, and this is due to slips of memory, to wilful alteration, when he thinks such alterations an improvement, and to extraneous influences—nervousness and the like.

Therefore the collector to give a true rendering of the original folk-melody should get as many notations of it as possible, and make such selection as his judgment and knowledge dictate. The ordinary simple "composed" tune generally continues throughout its length in one character of rhythm or time. The folk-air as sung to-day frequently ignores this rule, and may have passages in the middle of it which differ from the general run of the tune. The earlier collectors ignored this fact, and practically always placed such airs under one time signature, considering that any alteration of time-rhythm made by the singer was a grammatical error on his part. In some cases they were probably right, but recent comparisons of certain tunes, noted by different collectors in various parts of the country, go to prove that, to give particular effect to certain word passages, many folk-tunes have been composed with deliberate intention of breaking rhythm. The wary collector, therefore, while he is fully alive to the knowledge that folk-singers are not always to be relied upon for accurate transmission, is also aware of the fact I have above indicated.

IX. THE DIFFERENT CLASSES OF FOLK-SONG

THE folk-song that does, or did within recent years, exist is manifold in its variety. It reflects very accurately the type of thought that is, or was, current among the class who sang it. Its limits are strictly within their understanding, though now and again its commonplaces are tinged with romance. Yet this romance is not above the comprehension of the most humble and constitutes a grown-up's fairy tale.

It tells its story or voices its sentiment in the fewest possible words, and in tragedy is almost Biblical in narrative.

A consideration of a few of its types may be useful.

X. THE NARRATIVE BALLAD

THIS in its earliest form is, without doubt, the oldest surviving kind of folk-song. In all cases it is a long rhyming story which tells of events more or less romantic, and more or less true. It is probable that such ballads have come down to us from the middle ages, when professional gleemen, or minstrels, went from one noble house to another and sang such lyrics to the harp or to other accompaniment.

The stories are dramatic and sufficiently well-marked in character to be easily remembered. Obsolete expressions may be changed or may even remain, but the essentials of the story will be retained.

We have sufficient remnants on ballad sheets as well as in popular remembrance to show that there must have been an enormous number of these lyrical narratives in common currency. How long these had remained in oral transmission before being printed on ballad sheets is a question not easily answered. The question whether, in some instances, they were printed before being handed to the people may be answered in the affirmative in respect to a certain number of obviously later ballads.

The ballad-seller was bound to provide new wares for his patrons, and his trade could not go on without fresh material. Undoubtedly many of the ballads he printed were a re-dishing up of old stories, and many rhymesters, in default of newer ideas, fell back upon the Greek classic stories for subject. In fact, the common person of the sixteenth century might claim to be more familiar with the Homeric romance than the average "man in the street" of to-day. These can scarcely be called folk-ballads in the strictest sense, because they are evidently the work of people educated enough to put such matter from the classic, as well as from Italian authors, into doggerel verse.

The man of an earlier period was as anxious for novelty as he is to-day. The only difference is this—at the present time novelties so crowd upon him that they become stale very rapidly. In the "golden age" people gave leisurely consideration to and digested that which was put before them. Hence it was held tenaciously in memory, and ballads and tales lost none of their interest.

The invention of printing wrought a great change in every direction, and when the press gave forth the ballad-sheet it produced a new era in folk-singing. The ballad-sheet is so inextricably mixed up with the folk-song that, for a clear

THE NARRATIVE BALLAD 55

understanding, it will be necessary to devote some pages to it later on.

It is a noteworthy fact that among our ballad literature we find numbers of stories that are practically the same in other languages and current in other countries. If we find, as we frequently do, a ballad common amongst Scandinavian folk that is also known in England, or perhaps Brittany, we cannot safely determine its original birthplace, for there can be no doubt that popular folk-tales and ballads travelled from one country to another in a very remarkable degree.

Scotland has always been famous for her wealth of dramatic ballads. No man can read unmoved the many fine ballad narratives that are published in her ballad books, and without wondering whence came the rich flow of fancy and poetic beauty that inspired them.

In spite of all that has been written, much regarding the Scottish ballads remains a mystery. The early collectors appear to have had little scruple in regard to the ballads being printed exactly as received.

One thing we have satisfaction in, namely, that ballads of this character *did* exist, and that emendation of phrase, or addition of verse, affects the matter, on the whole, very little. The consideration of the Scottish ballad is, however, outside our inquiry, although some narrative lyrics that are commonly thought to have had origin in Scotland are found among English folk-singers. Of these, "Lammikin," collected by Miss Broadwood in Surrey, is a notable example, as also the different versions of "The Gipsy Laddie," and one or two others that may be found in the Folk-Song Society's Journals. Certainly the best-known narrative ballad among English folk-singers is "Lord Bateman," and versions of this exist in the Scottish ballad collections. "Barbara Allan" is another that has a Scottish variant, while the "Blind Beggar of Bethnal Green" seems to be entirely English. "Lord Thomas and Fair Eleanor," "The Outlandish Knight," "Geordie" are long ballads which, in a more or less fragmentary state, have been found in nearly every part of England.

One or two of the Robin Hood ballads have also been recovered from tradition, but such are, strangely enough, not common. All the tunes found united to the above-named narrative ballads appear to be ancient and contemporary with early versions of the words.

XI. LOVE SONGS AND MYSTIC SONGS

Love holds first place in all lyrics, and there is no exception to this rule in the folk-song. There is, however, this difference;—whilst the art-song is frequently couched in language abstract and sentimental, and enriched with metaphor and simile, the folk-song is almost always direct, and from its baldness of diction possessed of great force.

The declaration of love in a folk-song is simple, and there is no mincing of words. It is unmistakably fervent and in earnest. The tragedy of a girl's forsakenness is Biblical in its plainness; sometimes it is a song rather of triumph than pity.

Few more beautiful and direct specimens of the former type exist than the one beginning—

> "A brisk young farmer courted me,
>   He stole away my liberty,
> He stole my heart with my free goodwill,
>   I must confess I love him still.
>
> There is an ale-house in this town,
>   Where my love goes and sits him down;
> He takes another girl on his knee,
>   Ah! is not that a grief to me?

> A grief to me, I'll tell you why,
> Because she has more gold than I;
> Her gold will waste, her beauty blast,
> Poor girl she'll come like me at last ";

and so forth.

Another very beautiful love song is "The bonnie bonnie boy" noted by Miss Broadwood, and published in *English County Songs*. It opens—

> "I once loved a boy, a bonnie, bonnie boy,
> I loved him I'll vow and protest.
> I loved him so well, and so very, very well,
> That I built him a bower in my breast," etc.

A great feature in the love song of the folk-singer is the use of allegory. The words "thyme," "rue," the "broom," "barley," "wearing the green gown," and several other similes are freely used, and have an original meaning, for the most part, hidden from the modern singer. The ever popular "I sowed the seeds of love," in which is inextricably entangled that other song, "The sprig of thyme," is an inoffensive example of this type. The latter runs—

> "Come all you pretty fair maids
> That are just in your prime,
> I'd have you weed your garden clear
> And let no one steal your thyme.
>
> I once had a sprig of thyme,
> It prospered night and day;
> By chance there came a false young man
> And he stole my thyme away," etc.

MYSTIC SONGS

As can be well realised, examples of love songs could be given to any extent.

The folk-singer delights in something that gives a thrill of mysticism, and there are many having this characteristic in traditional remembrance. "The unquiet grave" is an example in point. It begins—

> "Cold blows the wind over my true love,
>   And cold blows the drops of rain.
> I never, never had but one true love,
>   And in the greenwood he was slain," etc.

"The Cruel Ship's Carpenter," and "The Nightingale" have each a ghost, as in a like manner has the one just quoted.

Of the mystic class is "The Prickly Bush." It is undoubtedly very old and is found in different forms among country singers. A copy occurs in *English County Songs*—

> "'O Hangman hold thy hand,' he cried,
>   'O hold thy hand awhile,
> For I can see my own dear father
>   Coming over yonder stile.
> Oh, the prickly, prickly bush,
> The prickly, prickly bush,
> It pricked my hand full sore;
> If ever I get out of the prickly bush,
> I'll never get in any more,'" etc.

Common all over the country, with place names that vary according to the district, is "The Lover's

Test," sometimes called "Scarborough Fair." The lover in this demands a cambric shirt made without needle and thread, and other impossibilities, with the reward that the lady shall then be his true love. The lady, equally ready, demands an acre of land between the sea foam and the sea sand. This is to be ploughed with a ram's horn, and to be sown all over with one peppercorn, and so on. When all this is done the lover can come for his cambric shirt. The story is a version of "The Elfin Knight," and of the same type as "Captain Wedderburn's Courtship."

XII. THE PASTORAL

THE pastoral song is fairly frequent, especially in the Southern counties of England. Its chief theme is the joys of country life. Such are the songs in which the ploughman is the chief personage, and one who glories in his calling. In *Sussex Songs* we find a very typical example—

"Come all ye jolly ploughboys, come listen to my lays,
    And join with me in chorus, I'll sing the ploughboy's praise.
    My song is of the ploughboy's fame,
    And unto you I'll relate the same,
    He whistles, sings, and drives his team,
        The brave ploughing boy."

THE PASTORAL

Then there are sheep-shearing songs, some of which may be seen in Dr Barrett's *English Folk-Songs* and elsewhere. *English County Songs* provides this ordinary example—

> " Our sheep shear is over, and supper is past;
> Here's a health to our mistress all in vull glaas,
> For she's a good 'ooman and purvides us good cheer,
> Here's a health to our mistress, so drink up your beer."

Other verses would, of course, provide for consumption of more beer by drinking the health of all the members of the family, and of such neighbours as the contents of the barrel allowed.

Harvest-home songs too are not lacking, and a small number take the form of a dialogue between a gardener and a ploughman, or between a husbandman and a serving-man.

A famous song well known among farm-labourers is that known as " Poor Old Horse," and of this there are several versions. This song probably suggested to Charles Dibdin his once popular song "The High-Mettled Racer," and to Thomas Bewick, the wood-engraver, his fine print of a worn-out horse in the rain called " Waiting for Death."

The ploughboy is sometimes in love and sings of his passion in the folk-song. Sometimes it is the lady who declares her love for the handsome ploughboy, and both varieties are quite popular specimens of rural simplicity.

XIII. DRINKING SONGS AND HUMOROUS SONGS

THE drinking song is not very common among folk-songs. "The good old leathern bottle," and some other South country songs, chiefly dealing with harvest home festivities, can scarcely be called such. They speak of the home-brewed farm ale in an honest fashion, and without the gloating over liquor which is so much a feature of the eighteenth century bacchanalian song. "When Joan's ale was new" is popular over most parts of England, and "Drink old England dry" is another very harmless production.

The humorous song does not very frequently occur. Sometimes we may come across one that fulfils all the essentials of wit but will scarcely bear repetition. Others are humorous and in other respects quite satisfactory. "Richard of Taunton Dean" is too well known to quote, and "The Dumb Wife Cured" is another that has been frequently reprinted, and it is possibly, really, not a folk-song. "The Grey Mare" is an excellent example. It tells of a young miller who made overtures to a young lady's father to obtain her hand. The dowry was agreed upon, save that the young man had fixed his mind upon the

HUMOROUS SONGS

farmer's grey mare as part of it. The old man not being inclined to part with this the bargain was "off." After the death of the farmer the miller again sought the lady, who declared she did not know him. Except that

> " A man in your likeness,
>   With long yellow hair,
>   *Did* once come a-courting
>   My father's grey mare."

"Eggs in the basket," narrating the adventures of two sailors, of which there are several versions in the *Folk-Song Journal*, comes under the category of humorous songs, and the Devonshire song "Widdicombe Fair" has, since its publication in *Songs of the West*, met with wide appreciation. Songs in dispraise of a married life are not frequent in folk-song, but there is a well-known one in " Advice to Bachelors," in Dr Barrett's *English Folk-Songs*, that appears to be a genuine folk-song. Its end verse contains the gist of the story. A criminal under the gallows is offered free pardon if he will marry, but—

> " He pondered deep, for life is dear,
>   But still he thought without a fear
>   That wives are cheap, and he knew well
>   How much his sorrows one might swell.

>   There's people here of every sort,
>   And why should I prevent their sport?
>   The bargain's hard in every part;
>   But the woman's the worst—
>   Drive on the cart!"

XIV. HIGHWAYMAN AND POACHER SONGS

IF the pressgang was an unpleasant factor in eighteenth century life, so also were the footpad and highwayman. The highwayman generally claimed the sympathy of the folk-song maker on the ground that—

"He never robbed a poor man upon the King's highway," and that his takings from the rich were distributed among the poor. This atoned for all crimes against person and property that were committed by such men as "Brennan on the Moor," the hero of a very favourite ballad. Sometimes these highwayman songs take a more moral tone, and the criminal, in the condemned cell, offers his fate as a warning to others. Charles Reilly, for example, sings—

>   "Adieu, adieu, I must meet my fate,
>   I was brought up in a tender state,
>   Until bad counsel did me entice
>   To leave off work, and follow vice.

POACHER SONGS

Which makes me to lament and say,
As in my doleful cell I lay,
'Pity the fall of young fellows all;
Ah well a day! Ah well a day!'
At seventeen I took a wife;
She was the joy of all my life,
And to maintain her rich and gay,
I went to rob on the King's highway,
  Which makes me to lament and say," etc.

Poaching was a matter so near the class that sang folk-songs that as a subject it could not fail in interest. If the folk-singer was not himself a poacher he was sufficiently in touch to feel a brotherly sympathy with him in his misfortunes, and in his triumphs, over the gamekeeper. As a consequence there are many poaching songs well known in rural districts, as—"Young Henry the poacher," "The Sledmere poachers," The death of Bill Brown," "Hares in the old plantation," etc.

Highway robbery and poaching led to execution and transportation, and both these are subjects for the folk-song maker. The execution songs appear, however, generally to be the work of professional ballad makers, and the "last dying speech and confession" of a criminal, with appended verses, was in print long before he had paid the penalty of his crime. The ballad was sung to one or other of those doleful tunes especially appropriated to this kind of song by the ballad chanter, who hawked the broadsides through the towns on the night of the execution. Frequently the tag to such ditties was—

> "Young men all now beware
> How you fall into a snare."

In a somewhat similar strain are the songs that tell of the miseries of transportation to Van Diemen's Land, for poaching or other offences.

XV. SOLDIER SONGS

OF soldier songs the folk-singer has comparatively few. One of the prettiest is that indifferently called "The Summer Morning," or "The White Cockade." It commences—

"It was one Monday morning, as I came o'er the moss,
I had no thought of listing till the soldiers did me cross;
They kindly did invite me to a flowing bowl, and down
They advancèd me some money, ten guineas and a crown.

'Tis true my love has 'listed; he wears a white cockade;
He is a handsome, tall young man, besides a roving blade;
He is a handsome young man, and he's gone to serve the King.
Oh! my very heart is breaking all for the love of him!"

SOLDIER SONGS

Another soldier's song popular among folk-singers is "Pretty Polly Oliver," or "Polly Oliver's Ramble."

"One night Polly Oliver lay musing in bed;
A comical fancy came into her head,
Neither father nor mother shall make me false prove,
I'll 'list for a soldier and follow my love."

Polly dresses herself in male attire, mounts her father's black gelding, and joins the regiment, with the captain of which she is in love.

Then we have the pathetic "Deserter."

"When first I deserted I thought myself free
Until my false comrade informed on me."

Another favourite is "The Gentleman Soldier," and yet another, "The bonny Scotch lad with his bonnet so blue." The battle of Waterloo gave rise to several long ballads descriptive of the fight, and these in their full integrity of twenty or thirty verses used, not long ago, to be remembered by old soldiers.

XVI. SEA SONGS

THESE have always been welcome among English singers, and our nation has a plenitude of fine ones. In folk-song they generally take a narrative form and treat of adventures with pirates, and the like. Examples of this type are "Paul Jones," "Ward the pirate," "Henry Martin," "The bold Princess Royal," and some others. The pressgang songs might, in a sense, go under the heading "sailor songs," and, certainly, the Chanty, but these are dealt with separately. "The Golden Vanity" is popular, so is "The Mermaid," and both are well known to modern singers. "The Greenland Whale Fishery" is a fine example of a genuine whaling ditty (see *A Garland of Country Songs*), and "All on Spurn Point" is a narrative of a wreck.

The charming song "Stowbrow," or the "Drowned Sailor," is chiefly known on the Yorkshire coast.

"The Cruel Ship's Carpenter" is a story of a murder and a ghost, which follows the murderer to sea and denounces him. "William Taylor" (of which a parody exists) is fairly well known.

"The Coasts of Barbary" is a fine sea song, and "The Indian Lass," "Just as the tide was flowing," "On board a man-of-war," "Outward bound," and "The bold privateers" are sea songs that are commonly known but can boast no great degree of antiquity. "Fair Phœbe and her dark-ey'd sailor," and "The broken token"—the one being a variation of the other—are songs that fall under the heading " Love Songs."

XVII. PRESSGANG SONGS

THESE have a greater dramatic effect than any other type before dealt with. In the eighteenth century, when the constant war with France demanded a supply of men to man the navy, the pressgang was a very vital thing in the lives of the humbler classes. The law empowered (under a press warrant) officers of the King's Navy to seize any man, with few exceptions, and then and there remove him to a King's ship to serve as a common sailor. Violence was freely used, and at dead of night whole villages were cleared of their male inhabitants, and husbands and bread-winners dragged away, never, in most cases, to return. Such occurrences were well within the memory of those only just passed away. With such happenings in their midst, the folk-song makers had no lack of thrilling and appealing material. The romantic element was not absent, for it was quite possible, as the folk-song generally makes it, for an irate father to bribe the pressgang for the removal of an undesirable young ploughman, and so put an end to the love passages that existed between his daughter and him, thus leaving the ground clear for a wealthier or more favoured suitor. Poetic justice is almost always satisfied in the song by the lady seeking her true love on shipboard, and, by the production of " gold," reclaiming him. "The Banks of Sweet Dundee," which is wide-spread and a universal favourite, affords an excellent example of the pressgang song.

The beautiful song beginning—

> " 'Twas early, early in the Spring
> My love was pressed to serve the King,"

and that one called "The Nightingale," are earlier in date and quite charming specimens of the class.

XVIII. HUNTING AND SPORTING SONGS

THE folk-singer does not lack songs dealing with the sports he loves. The fox- and hare-hunting songs are in a degree reflexes of the eighteenth century ones—of great compass, and of much allusion to the Greek gods. It is in these that Diana, Aurora and Phœbus figure so largely.

The folk-song that deals with hunting, generally

HUNTING SONGS

is local in its narrative, and tells of some particular famous fox hunt or hare hunt, naming every squire or yeoman farmer that joined in it. "The Fylingdale Foxhunt" in *Traditional Tunes* is a good and typical example. In the same work will be found "The White Hare" (a description of a hare hunt), and a song of a not very frequent type detailing a cock fight.

XIX. SONGS OF LABOUR

PRIMITIVE folk appear to have always had particular songs appropriate to specific kinds of labour. Such songs seem to have been traditionally associated with each class of work, and to have been used either to give a marked rhythm, by which the efforts of a number of people are united at a certain moment (as the pull upon a rope), or generally to lighten work, an effect which song certainly has. It is well known that girls in a weaving shop, or other factory, work twice as well and feel the strain lighter while they are singing in chorus some favourite song or hymn. Soldiers on the march are less tired if the men are allowed to sing, or while the band plays. The Irish regiments marched out of Brussels before Waterloo to the strains of the then popular Moore's "Melodies," "The Young May Moon" being among the favourites. The men of the North during the American Civil War were cheered by the song " John Brown's Body," and our own soldiers in South Africa sung, with deep meaning (considering that the Boers always managed to have the advantage of the crest of the hill), " All that ever I want is a little bit off the top." Every great river of the world has its boat-songs; in most cases used by the rowers as an aid to their work. Specimens of these river boat-songs have been noted in China, India, on the Nile, and elsewhere. The well-known "Canadian Boat Song," of Thomas Moore, was adapted by him from a chant he himself heard on the St Lawrence river, the original of which chant, by the way, differs materially from the version he published.

The Sea Chanty is too wide a subject to be dealt with in this small volume. Its purpose is to give time to the pull of a rope, the thrust against a capstan bar, or on occasions when the pumps have to be used. The "Chanty" may be almost spoken of as obsolete. Its real home was the sailing vessel, but, at the present day, steam does so much of what formerly was man's labour, that the chanty has almost died a natural death.

SONGS OF LABOUR

There were capstan, pumping, and hauling chanties, and those used in furling sail, apart from the sailors' songs pure and simple. The sea chanty was generally commenced by a leader—the chanty man, who would perhaps string a few extemporary rough rhymes together, fitted to a well-known tune, while the men joined in a recognised nonsense chorus as they did the pulling, thrusting, or other work required.

The Chanties mostly in evidence amongst the English, or English-speaking, sailors are "Whiskey for my Johnnie," "Haul the bowline," "We're all bound to go," "The Rio Grande," "Reuben Ranzo," "Tom's gone to Ilo," "Storm Along," "Lowlands," "Santa Anna," "Sally Brown," "Banks of Sacramento," and many others, copies of which, with most of the above, are to be found in the *Folk-Song Journals*. The fact cannot be ignored that there is decided American influence in most of the sea chanties, and that points to them being interchangeable between the English and the American sailor. The ships trading to San Francisco and other sailing vessels that took long voyages round the "Horn" were fit resting-places for the chanty. In former times, on the old man-of-war ships, a fiddler was frequently requisitioned, or the anchor was raised to the music of a fife.

Songs of occupation appear to have lingered

ENGLISH FOLK-SONG

longest, in the United Kingdom, in the Hebrides, and quite recently there have been published in the *Folk-Song Journal* a number of interesting examples collected by Miss Tolmie. Others have been obtained by Mrs Kennedy Fraser.

The boat songs, or "Iorrams," are a feature of Gaelic music, as are the "luinigs" sung by the women as songs to lighten work where there are a number of people employed at any one occupation.

Gaelic music and song is outside the scope of this manual; although the subject of the worksongs used in the Highlands and Islands of Scotland is here lightly referred to for the purpose of indicating to the student that such a class of song is still in existence in the British Isles.

XX. TRADITIONAL CAROLS

THAT a large number of carols existed in a purely traditional form was somewhat of a revelation, even to the folk-song collector, when Miss Lucy Broadwood, Mr Cecil Sharp, and Dr Vaughan Williams published their "finds" in the *Folk-Song Journal*. Mr Robin H. Legge, as early as 1890, or before, had collected a number of tradi-

TRADITIONAL CAROLS 75

tional carols in Cornwall, but his valuable manuscript collection of them was accidentally destroyed.

Some of the folk-carols that have lately been recovered embody curious legends, the origin of which is difficult to trace. "The Bitter Withy" is one of these, and of this particular carol several variants have been obtained, chiefly in the Midland Counties. The story is to the effect that the infant Jesus being reproached for His humble birth by His play-fellows, "lords' and ladies' sons," makes a bridge over water with the beams of the sun, and passes safely over; His companions who follow Him being drowned. His Mother, Mary, chides Him and whips Him with a bunch of the withy (willow) twigs. Jesus then lays a curse on the willow and ordains that it shall for ever be rotten at the heart.

Another singular carol noted by Miss Broadwood is "King Pharaoh." It was obtained from the singing of gypsies in Sussex. Another version as "King Herod and the Cock" was obtained by Mr Cecil Sharp, and earlier versions, as "The Carnel and the Crane," are to be found in Sandys' *Christmas Carols*, and elsewhere. A roasted cock that crows three times and corn which is in ear and ripened the same day are the chief points in the story, as miracles that occur to testify to the divine origin of the infant Christ.

"The Moon shines bright," "The Cherry-tree Carol," "The joys of Mary," with "God rest you merry gentlemen," are all folk-carols, but words and tunes have long been in print.

There are two different types of carol—the religious, dealing with the Holy Nativity, and the festive. "Here we come a-wassailing" is a folk-carol of the latter kind, and there are many others of this character. One of the best known, which is yet sung traditionally, is the carol which, from some cause, is named as belonging to Gloucestershire—

> "Wassail, wassail all over the town,
> Our toast it is white, and our ale it is brown,
> Our bowl it is made of the maplin tree,
> So here's good fellow, I'll drink to thee," etc.

The Gloucestershire rustics singing the song used formerly to go from house to house bearing a gaily decorated maple-wood potato bowl, which it was expected would be filled with liquor, or in lieu of this a contribution of money placed in the bowl.

The May-day carol exists in several different kinds. Copies are to be found in Dr Barrett's collection, *English County Songs*, and in several other works.

William Hone, in his *Ancient Mysteries*, 1822, speaks of the Christmas carols that were at that time annually printed in chap-books and on broadsides. He gives a list of eighty-nine of these, some of which are still remembered among folk-singers.

XXI. CHILDREN'S SINGING-GAMES

THE tunes used by children in the traditional singing-games rank as folk-music, and are always of the most simple and marked character. Having these qualities they are easily remembered, and capable of being passed from one generation of children to another with but little chance of corruption. Although certain games have the same rhymes and tunes in different parts of the country, yet there are others where the airs are not so fixed.

A very high antiquity has been allotted to the origin of these games. It is claimed that many are reflexes of pagan marriage and burial customs, and even of sacrificial rites. Into this question it is outside the province of this book to inquire, but whatever may be adduced as to the great age the games themselves possess, it seems doubtful whether any exceptional degree of antiquity can be safely assigned to the existing tunes, though

78   ENGLISH FOLK-SONG

they are all pretty and charming, and well worth preservation, apart from their antiquarian association.

Many collections of these singing-games have been published; details of these will be found in the bibliography. Miss A. G. Gilchrist, of Southport, has noted a very great number from children in different parts of the country. Her collection, up to the present, remains in manuscript.

A number of the singing-game tunes resemble in a greater or less degree certain published airs, as "Nancy Dawson," "Sheriff Muir," and some others. Whether the children have taken these airs for their games, or whether the composers of the printed tunes have gone to the children's games for inspiration, is a problem not easily solved.

XXII. THE BALLAD SHEET AND SONG GARLAND

WHEN the folk-song singer did not get his song by oral transmission he took it from a ballad sheet, or from those small collections of songs which, for at least three centuries, were called "Garlands." The words of most of our folk-songs were gener-

THE BALLAD SHEET 79

ally printed either on the ballad sheet (otherwise "broadside"), or included among those that formed the contents of the "Garland," and nowhere else, except in the rarest instances. Regular song books were too dignified to admit songs or ballads of the folk-song class. As a consequence the folk-songs that survive in an early printed form are chiefly found on broadsides.

Technically, the broadside is a printed piece of paper (the size is immaterial) meant to be read unfolded. A tradesman's hand-bill, for example, is a broadside. Folded, the broadside becomes folio, quarto, or octavo. The "garlands" were small folded booklets of either eight or sixteen pages, and contained ten or twelve songs, the outer page being generally decorated with a woodcut, and having a list of the songs contained within.

The reason why the broadside ballad was printed on one side only appears to be this—It was the practice to paste them on cottage walls, inside cupboard doors, chest lids, and such like places. There are many references in literature to this method of displaying the ballad, as for example—

"I will now lead you to an honest ale-house where we shall find a cleanly room, lavender in the window, and twenty ballads stuck about the wall."—Walton's *Compleat Angler*, 1653.

No wonder that the old angler and his pupil found so many delightful snatches of quaint old song current where ballads and songs were so fostered. The *Spectator* shows that the usage had not died out in Queen Anne's reign—

"I cannot for my heart leave a room before I have thoroughly studied the walls of it, and examined the several printed papers which are usually pasted upon them."—No. 85, vol. ii.

Although the ballad was freely hawked about the streets of towns, and carried into the country by "flying stationers" and pedlars (witness Autolycus in the *Winter's Tale*), yet the pastings upon walls and the constant foldings of loose ballad sheets soon destroyed existing copies, for few of the old ballad lovers were like Mr Pepys and Captain Cox. Laneham, it will be remembered, tells in his "Letter," 1575, describing the festivities at Kenilworth Castle, that Cox's ballads numbered more than a hundred, and were "all ancient," and were "fair wrapt in parchment, and tied with a whip cord." Would there had been more of the Captain's careful disposition.

Broadside ballads must have come among the people with the first dawn of printing, and in Henry the Eighth's reign they had become of such weight in political influence that one or more royal edicts were levied against them. The

BROADSIDE BALLADS 81

earliest known English printed ballad is, in date, about 1540. Ballad printing was generally done by small local printers, or else by those larger London printers who made a speciality of the work, and who supplied the whole country with ballads and with "garlands."

Gough, Redman, Bankes, Walley, and many others who worked in London during the sixteenth century were noted printers of ballads. In the seventeenth century ballad printing became more general, and many of the publishers clubbed together, so that we find several names on one imprint. Henry Gosson printed in 1616, and John Trundle, his contemporary, was so noted as a ballad vendor that he is named in Ben Jonson's play, "Every Man in His Humour." In 1642 Francis Coles (or Coules) flourished and issued ballads in conjunction with William Gilbertson, having a shop on Saffron Hill. Of this period also were Alexander Milbourn, Francis Grove, J. Wright, William Onley, and the "Assignees of Thomas Symcocke." At a later date William Thackeray, at the "Angel in Duck Lane," issued, with Passenger, at the "Three Bibles on London Bridge," many interesting ballads, garlands, and chap-books. One of their dates is 1687.

All these seventeenth century ballads, or the chief part of them, were printed in "𝔟𝔩𝔞𝔠𝔨-𝔩𝔢𝔱𝔱𝔢𝔯,"

F

a type of Gothic character which was specially reserved for law books, bibles, and romances long after its discontinuance as ordinary text. They were generally printed on rather large paper, about 14 inches by 10 inches, and, of course, only on one side of the paper. The name of the tune was frequently given, and on some a few musical notes, professing to be the tune, were appended to the verses. These musical notes, however, were a fraudulent inducement to purchasers, for they were merely set at random. Rude woodcuts, which more or less illustrated the theme of the ballad, generally headed the whole.

The most noted collections of this period of ballad are the Roxburghe collection in the British Museum, and the Pepysian at Cambridge. It must be pointed out that a great number of these ballads were scarcely folk-songs—that is, they were not "born of the people"—and only a certain proportion were current among them. There were professional ballad writers who supplied rhymed narratives to order for the ballad seller, not only upon topical events, but re-dishings of earlier romances, and other matter.

Whether at the opening of the eighteenth century printed ballads began to be out of favour, or whether the ballads have not been so carefully

BALLAD PRINTERS

preserved, is not quite clear, but they are certainly more rare of this period.

The chief ballad printer of this date was John Cluer, who was printing ballads in 1720, and shortly after this date was established as a music publisher of repute. He worked in Bow Church Yard, Cheapside, and was succeeded by William Dicey, who had been in partnership with Robert Raikes, at Northampton, in the ballad and chap-book printing business. Robert Raikes removed to Gloucester, where he established the first Gloucester newspaper. He was father to Robert Raikes, the originator of Sunday Schools.

An important range of ballad sheets were those which issued from the Aldermary Church Yard press. In 1793 J. Marshall was at this address, printing engraved song sheets with pictorial headings. There was also a J. Marshall at Newcastle-on-Tyne, who published song garlands about 1820.

One of the best-known ballad printers at the end of the eighteenth century was John Evans, of 42 Long Lane, Smithfield. He printed broadside ballads, chap-books, and garlands. He and his sons at a later date printed for the Religious Tract Society, producing such quaint religious stories as *The Shepherd of Salisbury Plain*. The Evans family, and successors, were in full vigour as printers as late as 1815.

It was at the beginning of the nineteenth century that the great ballad printer J. Pitts appeared. It is said that "Johnny Pitts" was a female who had been a bumboat woman. The ballad sheets that issued from the Pitts' press are all of interest, and many genuine folk-songs appear on them. A rival to Pitts came from Alnwick in the person of James Catnach, the son of a printer in that small Northumbrian town. James Catnach first commenced business in 1813, at 2 and 3 Monmouth Court, Seven Dials, and he made a complete revolution in ballad-sheet printing. The early ballad-mongers used a rough grey, or blue tinted, paper and their type was none of the best, or clearest. Catnach changed the shape of the ballad sheet into Large Post Quarto (about 10 × 8 inches), used good, though thin, white paper, and clear type. Many of his wood-blocks were either by the Bewick brothers, or by their pupils. He put forth an enormous quantity of ballads and songs, and seems to have not only employed men to write songs on topical events, but also to have for the first time put into print many a stray folk-song which the ballad-singers, who flocked to buy his ballads, would recite to him. This latter fact accounts for a certain amount of ignorant mistakes that occur in the text.

After founding an immense business he retired

BALLAD PRINTERS

in 1838, and died in 1841. His married sister, Anne Ryle, took over the business and advertised that she had "4000 sorts" of ballad sheets. Her manager, James Paul, appears to have been some sort of an editor for her, and it is believed that he wrote, or re-wrote, certain of the ballads and songs she printed. He was, with others, proprietor of the business at one time, but finally it became the property of W. S. Fortey, who reprinted from Catnach's old stereotypes. T. Batchelor, Piggot, and T. Birt were other ballad printers, a little later than Catnach.

The broadsides printed by Henry Such are of considerable interest to the collector, as they contain versions of folk-songs which are generally good. He was printing in 1849, and his successors of the same surname reprinted his ballad sheets up to a recent date. Provincial ballad-sheet printers are Walker of Durham (flourishing in 1839), and Harkness of Preston, of a somewhat later date. R. Barr of Leeds and J. Bebbington of Manchester were broadside printers of forty or fifty years ago, while Shelmerdine & Co. of Manchester date from about 1815.

The folk-song collector cannot ignore the ballad sheet, for upon it are found the words of many folk-songs of which he may only obtain very fragmentary versions from the singer. It is not to be understood that the ballad sheet version of a folk-song is always an accurate one, but it is worth having, for the folk-song singer has generally learned his words, or at any rate refreshed his memory, from the broadside copy.

The ballad printer was too wise a business man to print on the sheet *only* folk-songs. He printed a popular lyric side by side with an old traditional song, for the sheet had room for at least two sets of verses, and he, by this means, catered for two classes of customers.

BIBLIOGRAPHY

THE following works have each a bearing upon English Folk-Song and Folk-Music, and the student will find a reference to them of great help in obtaining a full knowledge of the subject. Many others might have been named, for it is difficult, if not impossible, to fix a limit for the bibliography of a particular line of study.

COLLECTION OF BALLADS AND SONGS, WITHOUT MUSIC

ASHTON, JOHN. A Century of Ballads. Collected, edited, and illustrated in facsimile by ———. 1887.

—— Modern Street Ballads. 1888.

—— Real Sailor Songs.

BIBLIOGRAPHY 87

BALLAD SOCIETY, THE. Published between 1868 and 1881 many volumes of ballads which were reprinted from the black letter broadsides in the British Museum and elsewhere.

BALLADS, THE ROXBURGHE. A Book of Roxburghe Ballads. Edited by J. Payne Collier. 1847.

—— Edited by Charles Hindley. 2 vols. 1874.
(These two publications are merely selections from the collection.)

BELL, JOHN. Rhymes of Northern Bards; being a curious collection of old and new songs and poems peculiar to the counties of Newcastle-upon-Tyne, Northumberland, and Durham. 1812.

BELL, ROBERT. Early Ballads illustrative of History, Tradition, and Custom. Edited by ——. 1856.

—— Ancient Poems, Ballads, and Songs of the Peasantry of England. Edited by ——. 1857
(Of these two most useful volumes many later editions have been published. They were really compiled and annotated by John Henry Dixon, and originally appeared in 1846, with some slight differences, as one of the publications of the Percy Society. As they formed one of the series of "Bell's English Poets," the general editor's name appeared instead of the real compiler's. Other volumes of the Percy Society's publications have some interest for the inquirer into English folk-song.)

CHILD, F. J. English and Scottish Ballads. Selected and edited by ——. 8 vols. 1857-1859.
(This is the original American edition. A later edition was published in 1861, and finally a large quarto edition with much new matter was begun in 1882, and completed in 1898 in 10 parts. A condensed edition of Child's ballads was issued in 1904.)

88 ENGLISH FOLK-SONG

CLARK, ANDREW. The Shirburn Ballads, 1585-1616. Reprinted from the MS by ——. 1907.

EVANS, THOMAS. Old Ballads, historical and narrative, with some of modern date. 2 vols. 1777.

(A later edition in 4 vols, 1784. A different and fuller edition, 1810, 4 vols.)

HARLAND, JOHN. Ballads and Songs of Lancashire. Chiefly older than the nineteenth century. 1865.

JEWITT, L. Ballads and Songs of Derbyshire, with illustrative notes and examples. 1867.

LILLY, JOSEPH. A collection of seventy-nine black letter ballads and broadsides printed in the reign of Queen Elizabeth. 1867.

(This is a reprint from a collection of broadsides that formerly belonged to George Daniels, the antiquary.)

LOGAN, W. H. A Pedlar's Pack of ballads and songs. 1869.

PERCY, BISHOP. Reliques of Ancient English Poetry, consisting of old heroic ballads, songs, and other pieces of popular poetry. 3 vols. 1765.

(Second edition, 1767; third, 1775; fourth, 1794; and numerous later editions.)

—— Folio Manuscript. A reprint by Hales and Furnivall of this celebrated collection from which the "Reliques" were selected. 4 vols. 1867-1868.

RIMBAULT, DR E. F. A little book of songs and ballads, gathered from ancient musick books, MS. and printed. 1851.

RITSON, JOSEPH. Ancient Songs and Ballads from the reign of Henry the Second. 2 vols. 1787.

(Later editions, 1790, 1792, and 1829.)

RITSON, JOSEPH. Northern Garlands. 1810. A reprinted edition, 1887.

(They consist of four song "Garlands" issued by Joseph Ritson. "The Bishopric Garland or Durham Minstrel," 1784—enlarged edition, 1792; "The Yorkshire Garland," 1788; "The Northumberland Garland," 1793; and "The North Country Chorister," 1802.)

—— Robin Hood, a collection of all the ancient poems, songs, and ballads now extant relative to that celebrated English outlaw. 2 vols. 1795.

(Collections of the Robin Hood ballads reprinted from Ritson's work are innumerable. An excellent edition appeared in 1820, and again in 1823, while a very useful one was published by Griffin about 1850.) Another reprint was issued in 2 vols. in 1884.

SHARP, Sir CUTHBERT. The Bishopric Garland of Legends, Songs, Ballads, etc., belonging to the county of Durham. 1834.

SIDGWICK, FRANK. Popular Ballads of the Olden Time. First to fourth series, 1903-1912.

(See also several small carol books compiled by the above.)

ENGLISH FOLK-SONG COLLECTIONS WITH THE TUNES, OR MUSICAL WORKS BEARING ON THE SUBJECT

CHAPPELL, WM. National English Airs. 2 vols. 1838-1839.

—— Popular Music of the Olden Time. 2 vols. 1856-1859.

(The new edition of Chappell's "Popular Music" edited by H. E. Wooldridge was published in 1893, but the traditional airs obtained by Chappell and his friends are omitted.)

RIMBAULT, EDWARD F. Musical Illustrations of Bishop Percy's Reliques of Ancient English Poetry. A collection of old ballad tunes chiefly from rare MSS. and early printed books. 1850.

—— Nursery Rhymes. Edited and arranged by E. F. Rimbault. (Several editions.) Chappell.

MASON, Miss M. A. Nursery Rhymes and Country Songs. 1877.

(A reprint by Metzler, recently issued.)

BRUCE, Dr C., and J. STOKOE. Northumbrian Minstrelsy: Ballads, Melodies, and Pipe Tunes of Northumbria. 1882.

STOKOE, JOHN, and SAMUEL REAY. Songs and Ballads of Northern England.

(Contents principally taken from "Northumbrian Minstrelsy" harmonised by the late Mr S. Reay, about 1895.)

SUMNER, HEYWOOD. The Besom Maker, and other country folk-songs. 1888.

SMITH, LAURA A. Music of the Waters. 1888.

—— Through Romany Song-land. 1889.

BROADWOOD, Rev. JOHN. Sussex Songs, arranged by H. F. Birch Reynardson. 1889.

(This is a reprint of the tunes collected and privately issued in 1843 by the Rev. John Broadwood, with additional ones collected by Miss Lucy E. Broadwood.)

BARING-GOULD, Rev. SABINE. Songs and Ballads of the West. A collection made from the mouths of the people, by Rev. S. Baring-Gould and Rev. H. Fleetwood Sheppard. 4 parts. 1889-1891. Methuen.

(Several later editions of the parts, and in volume form. Also an entirely new edition in association with Mr Cecil J. Sharp, published 1905.)

—— A Garland of Country Songs. 1895.

BIBLIOGRAPHY

KIDSON, FRANK. Old English Country Dances gathered from scarce printed collections, and from manuscript. 1890.
(Contains several hitherto unprinted folk-airs used as dance tunes.)

—— Traditional Tunes: a collection of ballad airs, chiefly obtained in Yorkshire and the South of Scotland. 1891.

BARRETT, W. ALEX. English Folk-Songs. Collected and arranged by W. A. Barrett. Novello. 1891.

BROADWOOD, LUCY E., and J. A. FULLER MAITLAND. English County Songs. Collected and edited by ——. Leadenhall Press, and Cramer. 1893.

—— English Traditional Songs and Carols. Boosey. 1908.

TOZER, F. Sailors' Songs and Chanties. Words by F. Davis, music arranged from traditional sailors' airs. Boosey.

BRADFORD, J., and A. FAGGE. Old Sea Chanties. Collected and arranged by ——. Metzler.

GRAHAM, JOHN. Dialect Songs of the North. Collected and edited by ——. Curwen.

SHARP, CECIL J. Folk-Songs from Somerset, gathered and edited with pianoforte accompaniments by Cecil J. Sharp (and Rev. Charles L. Marson). 1905.
(Four more parts afterwards added. In the fourth and fifth parts Mr Sharp's name alone appears as editor.)

—— Folk-Song Airs. Collected and arranged for the pianoforte by ——. Books I. and II. Novello.

—— A School Series of Folk-Songs, in numbers. Novello.

BARING-GOULD, Rev. S., and CECIL J. SHARP. English Folk-Songs for Schools. 1906. Curwen.

FOLK-SONGS OF ENGLAND. Novello.
Book I. Folk-Songs from Dorset. Collected by H. E. D. Hammond.
Book II. Folk-Songs from the Eastern Counties. Collected by R. Vaughan Williams.
Book III. Folk-Songs from Hampshire. Collected by George B. Gardiner.

FOLK-SONG SOCIETY, JOURNALS OF. 18 parts have been issued. (Hon. Sec., 19 Berners Street.)

CAROLS

GILBERT, DAVIES. Some Ancient Christmas Carols with the tunes to which they were formerly sung. 1822. Second edition, 1823.
(The tunes are eight in number.)

SANDYS, WILLIAM. Christmas Carols, Ancient and Modern, including the most popular in the West of England. 1833.

—— Christmastide: its history, festivities and carols. *c.* 1852.

RIMBAULT, E. F. Christmas Carols. Edited and arranged by ——. Chappell.

HUSK, W. H. Songs of the Nativity, being Christmas Carols old and new. *c.* 1865.

HELMORE, THOMAS. Christmas Carols. Novello. 1853.

BRAMLEY, Rev. H. R., and STAINER, JOHN. Christmas Carols old and new. *c.* 1868. Reprinted in two small editions with a third series added. Novello.

BIBLIOGRAPHY

FULLER MAITLAND, J. A. English Carols of the Fifteenth Century, from a MS. roll in the library of Trinity College, Cambridge, with added parts by W. S. Rockstro.

DUNCOMBE, W. D. V. A Collection of Old English Carols as sung at Hereford Cathedral. Weekes.

HILL, Rev. GEOFFRY. Wiltshire Folk-Songs and Carols. 1904.

BROADWOOD, LUCY E. English Traditional Songs and Carols. Boosey. 1908.

SHARP, CECIL J. English Folk-Carols. Novello. 1911.

GILLINGTON, ALICE. Old Christmas Carols of the Southern Counties. Curwen.

SHAW, MARTIN, and PERCY DEARMER. The English Carol Book. 1913.

SINGING-GAMES

GOMME, ALICE B. Traditional Games of England, Scotland, and Ireland. 2 vols. 1894-1898.

—— Children's Singing-Games, with the tunes to which they are sung. Oblong. 2 series. 1894.

—— Old English Singing-Games.

KIDSON, FRANK, and ALFRED MOFFAT. Eighty Singing-Games, old, new, and adapted. Bayley & Ferguson.

GILLINGTON, ALICE E. Old Hampshire Singing-Games.

—— Old Isle of Wight Singing-Games.

—— Old Surrey Singing-Games. Curwen.

LITERATURE

ECKENSTEIN, LINA. Comparative Studies in Nursery Rhymes. 1906.

ENGEL, CARL. The Study of National Music. 1866.

—— The Literature of National Music. 1879.

GLYN, MARGARET H. Analysis of the Evolution of Musical Form. 1909.

HALLIWELL, JAMES ORCHARD. The Nursery Rhymes of England, obtained principally from Oral Tradition. 1843.
(A reprint from the volume contributed to the Percy Society's publications by Halliwell in 1841. A most valuable work, several times, with the addition of "Nursery Tales," re-issued.)

MUSICAL ASSOCIATION, PROCEEDINGS OF. For 1904-1905-1907-1908.
(These years contain different papers on folk-music.)

SHARP, CECIL J. English Folk-Songs: Some Conclusions. 1907.

ENGLISH FOLK-DANCE
BY MARY NEAL

ACKNOWLEDGMENTS

Acknowledgment is given with many thanks to—

Miss LUCY BROADWOOD, who directed attention to several works of reference.

Miss A. G. GILCHRIST, for permission to use the music of the Moston rush-bearing Morris dance and for pointing out its connection with "To-morrow shall be my dancing day."

Miss NELLIE CHAPLIN, for allowing me to use her copy of *Playford's Dancing Master*.

Mr CLIVE CAREY, for reading proofs and other help.

Mr WALTER DODGSON, for translating passages from *Mysterium und Mimus im Rigveda* by Leopold von Schroeder.

Mr BRASSINGTON, of the Stratford-on-Avon Memorial Library, for help in looking up works of reference.

Mr JOHN GRAHAM, for suggesting works of reference.

Mr JOHN BECK, for lending *Kemp's Morris Dance Wonder*.

Sir J. G. FRAZER, whose work, *The Golden Bough*, is indispensable to the study of folk-dance.

The Daily Chronicle, for permission to reproduce the pictures of the Bampton dancers.

Messrs CURWEN & SONS, for permission to reproduce two pictures from the *Espérance Morris Books*.

Morris Dancers at Bampton-in-the-Bush, Oxon.

INTRODUCTION

BEFORE the year 1905 few people knew that England possessed a traditional folk-dance of her own, and fewer still realised that the national dances were still practised on certain festival occasions in several villages and country towns, for the most part in the Midland and Northern counties. The word "folk" when used to describe a dance may be interpreted in two ways. It may be used to signify a dance (either traditional or not) at one time popular amongst the people, or its meaning may be limited to those dances whose origin is lost in antiquity and which have been passed on from generation to generation by unlettered folk without the aid of written music or written instruction as to steps or evolutions. That this book may be of more use to those who wish either to study the available English dances or to pass them on to the present generation, the wider meaning of the word "folk" will be understood.

But a very marked distinction must be drawn between the two classes of folk-dance, between those recorded in books and still danced by peasant folk as a merely social dance, with no special significance beyond being an occasion for the display of gallantry, coquetry, and the courtesies of social intercourse; and those dances, until lately unrecorded, which are religious in origin and are the expression in rhythm of primitive beliefs and magical ceremonial.

In the former are included the country dances and certain popular court dances. The latter include the Sword dances, Morris dances, the Furry dance, and Horn dance. As the origin of all dancing may be directly or indirectly traced to the ceremonial of primitive religions, it will be well first of all to give some account of those traditional dances still lingering in English villages which give unmistakable signs of their origin.

The primitive forms of the traditional dance can only be guessed at by the student of to-day, for probably every epoch, every generation, and every individual dancer has added to, modified, or taken from the original dance, but enough is still with us to make the study an intensely interesting one both from the archæological and from the social point of view.

The most important surviving traditional dance in England to-day is undoubtedly the Morris dance, both because of the far greater number of Morris dances still in existence and because of the greater differences between the individual dances. But

INTRODUCTION

very closely allied to, if not identical with, the Morris is the Sword dance, and again allied to both is the Mummers' play.

My own experience in talking to country dancers coincides with that of Mr Cecil Sharp, who says that if you ask a sword dancer of Grenoside or Earsdon, he will insist that he is a Morris dancer, and that one is often sent after a Morris dance, only to find traces of a Mummers' play. He adds, "In due course it will dawn upon him (the collector) that the sword dancer of Northern England, the Morris dancer of the Midlands and the South, and the Mummer of all England and Scotland are in the popular view as one and pass under the same name." And it is the word "Morris" which gives the clue to the origin and nature of the dance, whatever the precise form which it takes.

With one exception the dictionaries and glossaries I have consulted derive the word "Morris" from "Moorish." Mr Cecil Sharp says that the weight of testimony must be held to show Morocco as the fount and origin of the dance,[1] but Mr John Graham and Mr Kidson throw doubt on its Moorish origin. The fact that the Morisco, supposed to be the counterpart of the English Morris, was a solo dance performed with

[1] Later, I believe, Mr Sharp changed his opinion.

INTRODUCTION

resemblance between the dances of the Salii and the English Morris and sword dances, and this resemblance adds to the evidence in favour of our traditional dance having originated in sun worship and nature worship generally.

The following description of the Salii from *The Golden Bough* will illustrate this point:—"As priests of Mars, the god of Agriculture, the Salii probably had also certain agricultural functions. They were named from the remarkable leaps which they made. Now we have seen that dancing and leaping high are common sympathetic charms to make the crops grow high. Was it one of the functions of the Salii to dance and leap on the fields at the spring or autumn sowing, or at both?

"The dancing procession of the Salii took place in October as well as in March, and the Romans sowed both in spring and autumn. The weapons borne by the Salii, while effective against demons in general, may have been especially directed against the demons who steal the seed corn in the ripe grain. In Western Africa the field labours of tilling and sowing are sometimes accompanied by dances of armed men in the fields."

In a footnote the author also throws out a suggestion that, as the Salii were said to have been founded by Morrius, King of Veii, and this seems to be etymologically the same as Mamurius and

Mars, the word "Morris" may be the same. In answer to a query, however, he does not appear to take this as a really serious suggestion.[1]

The following are some of the reasons for connecting the Morris dance with primitive religious customs:—

(1) The characteristic of the processional form of the dance as performed by the living dancers to-day is a slow, dignified rhythmic movement, which is very marked in the Bampton (Oxon.) dancers, who have an unbroken tradition going back some hundreds of years.

The set dances display a much more lively character and are characterised by wild leaps, twirlings round, hand-clapping, stick clashing, and the waving of handkerchiefs, so that we can easily imagine the present Morris as a descendant of the solemn processional up the mountain-side to greet the morning sun, and the scenes of wild joy on the summit at the appearance of the source of light and life to his waiting worshippers.

[1] L. von Schroeder in *Mysterium und Mimus im Rigveda* (p. 113) suggests, following A. Kuhn, that the root of the word "Morris" is the same as that of Maruts, the band of dancing warriors attendant upon Indra.

INTRODUCTION 103

(2) Many of the Morris and Sword dancers have evolutions which are characteristic of ceremonial used by savage people in the worship of the sun. The Abingdon (Berks) dances, a very old tradition, end with a complete circle. Bean-setting, one of the Headington (Oxon.) dances, begins with two half-circles danced in opposite directions. The Bampton dances have circles, half-circles, and gypsies, another form of circle. The Gloucestershire dances have the same. In some dances the dancers advance and retire into the centre, forming a widening and narrowing circle alternately, all of which illustrate by mimetic action the supposed movements of the sun and the sun's rays. All were probably actuated by mimetic magic, primitive man believing that by imitating the rising and setting of the sun and by lighting fires he actually caused the return of the sun to the earth.

(3) The appearance in different forms of the King and Queen, the Lord and Lady, the Mayor and Squire in the ceremonial of the dance. These figures indubitably link up the dances with those ceremonies attending the crowning of the King of the

Wood, who, representing the life of the earth's vegetation, was yearly slain lest his vigour might wane and all the green life of earth perish with it. The slaying of this King and the revels which preceded it and the crowning of the fresh and younger Monarch were all still dimly to be traced in many revels and dances in English villages within quite recent years.

At Abingdon, the story runs, two hundred years ago a great fight took place between the dwellers in Ock Street and the rest of the burghers of the town. The Ock Street people outnumbering the rest of the whole town thought they had the right to appoint a Mayor. A beast was slain in the market-place and roasted whole, a fight took place for the horns, and the winning side then carried the horns in the Morris dancing round the town. The horns are in existence to-day and are carried by the Mayor of the Morris accompanied by the Squire carrying a Sword. There are traces left still of the gold used to tip the horns which are mounted on a bull's head, with flaming red nostrils, thus making it evident that the beast was regarded as sacred. These ceremonies took place on St John the Baptist's Eve, celebrating the summer solstice.

Abingdon Dancers, whose tradition goes back to 1700

(*The Squire' holding the sword, wooden cup, and collection box, also the pole on which is mounted the bull's head and horns formerly carried by the Mayor of the Morris*)

At Kirtlington it was customary for the dancers to conduct ceremonially a young maiden from her father's house early in the morning. She must be of spotless reputation, and dressed in white with floating blue ribbons. She stayed with the dancers until night fell, when she was taken back to her father's house. During the time she was with the dancers she was regarded as sacred, and anyone who so much as jostled her in the crowd must pay a fine of half a crown. Later a lamb substituted for the maiden was decorated with flowers and ribbons, carried round by the dancers, and at intervals put down while they danced round about it in a circle.

At Kidlington (Oxon.) Blount describes a similar ceremony. "The Monday after Whitsun week a fat lamb was provided, and the maidens of the town having their thumbs tied together were permitted to run after it, and she who with her mouth took hold of the lamb was declared the Lady of the Lamb, which was killed, cleaned, and with the skin hanging on it was carried on a pole before the lady and her companions to the green attended with music and a Morisco dance of men and another of women. The rest of the day was spent in mirth and merry glee. Next day the lamb, partly baked, partly boiled and partly roasted, was served up for the lady's feast, when she sat majestically at the upper end of the table and her companions, with the music playing during the repast, which having finished the solemnity ended."

In most places where there are still lingering traces of the Morris there also linger these traces of the ancient sacrifice of the King of the Wood, and of the Worship of the Sun.

Another link with the festivals of ancient religions seems to be the constant use of a mask in the traditional dance, or the disguising of the face with black, white, or red paint. In *The Golden Bough* Sir James Frazer gives an account of a pagan festival which may possibly account for this survival.

"In Mexico a Woman who represented the Mother of the Gods, the Earth Goddess, after being feasted and entertained by sham fights for some days was beheaded on the shoulders of a man. The body was flayed, and one of the men clothing himself in the skin became the representative of the goddess Toci. The skin of the thigh was removed separately, and the young man who represented the Maize god, the son of the goddess Toci, wrapt it round his face as a mask. Various ceremonies then followed in which the two men clad in the woman's skin played the parts respectively of god and goddess."

INTRODUCTION

To-day in England curious hints still survive which show that the simple country folk never altogether lost the feeling that these dances were not quite ordinary, but represented some sort of magic charm with which it would be unsafe to interfere. Mr Sidney O. Addy, in his *Household Tales*, says:—" At Curbar, in Derbyshire, it is said that Morris dancing is really fairy dancing, and that 'Morris dancing' means 'fairy dancing.' Morris dancers of the present day (1895), it is said, go through the same form of dancing that the fairies go through, except that of course they cannot perform such intricate figures as the fairies can. The figures which the Morris dancers of the present day go through are very elaborate and very difficult to learn. A man said to me 'that Morris dancing had been taken away from the fairies.' There is something beautiful and strange in the music to which the Morris dancers dance. If ever music was not of this world it is this. To hear it is to believe that Morris dancing was a religious rite."

The following extract seems to link up our English Morris dance with the Moorish dance, so that whether we choose to derive the word "Morris" from the Keltic Mor-uiseil, or from the Moorish, or whether we think that the similarity of the two words made a confusion in the popular mind, and so the two kinds of dances came to be known by one name, we can still hold the belief that the English traditional dance which has come to us down the ages was originally a religious dance celebrating the return of the Sun-god and the sowing and the gathering of the crops on which man's life depended.

Mr Addy asks:—"Has it (the Morris dance) descended to us from a dusky Iberian people, once a distinct caste in England, in whose magical powers and religion the dominant races believed? In his dictionary, Professor Skeat has concluded that a Morris dancer was a Moorish dancer. Assuming that such is the case, we may ask ourselves why these dances were so called. Are we to suppose that English peasants borrowed the dance from the Moors in historical times? Or are we to believe that it was handed down in England from an early period by the remnants of a dark-coloured Iberian people who, according to Tacitus, crossed over from Spain and were, in fact, Moors? In Yorkshire, a rude Christmas play known as the Peace Egg is performed. In that play the chief act is the slaughter by St George of England of a Black Prince of Paladine whom St George stigmatises as a 'Black Morocco Dog.' The play seems to represent an old feud between a light-haired and a dark-haired people once inhabiting

England: and it may be that in popular speech the dark-haired people were once known as Moors. If this dramatised contest between St George of England and the 'Black Morocco Dog' does not point back to a time when conflicts existed in this country between a dusky race of Iberian or Moorish origin and a light-haired people which conquered and enslaved them, to what can we ascribe its origin? We can only say that this play is of historical or literary and not of traditional origin. But the form of the play renders an historical or literary origin impossible, and the whole performance seems to be nothing else but a rude and popular reminiscence of an ancient national feud.

"It seems relevant to mention here an old earthwork, extending for some miles in length near Sheffield, known in one part of its course as Barber Balk. The direction of the earthwork is from south-west to north-east, and the ditch is uniformly on the southern side, as if it had been intended as a defence against attack from that side. Some modern scholars identify the Barbars or Berbers, a people inhabiting the Saracen countries along the north coast of Africa, with the Iberians. Can it be that an invading Celtic people threw up this earthwork as a defence against a dusky Iberian foe coming from the south, and that the ancient name of the earthwork has been handed down from a remote time, thereby preserving its true history? And is it not possible that the Iberians, the Morris or Moor, the 'Black Morocco Dog' of the traditional play and the Barber are identical?

"A great authority on early Britain 'has accepted and employed the theory advanced by ethnologists that the early inhabitants of this country were of Iberian origin.'"

The fact that the Morris dancers sometimes blackened their faces need not necessarily mean that they wish to represent the Moors, but that they were thought to represent Moors because their faces were blackened.

The Morris dance was called in some places the Northern lights and the Aurora Borealis because of its desultory movements, and it may have been this which inspired Milton to write—

> "The sounds and seas, with all their finny drove,
> Now to the Moon in wavering Morrice move."

If, as I have tried to show, the traditional dance is part of an ancient religious ceremonial dating from pre-Christian days, we shall not be surprised to find that in Early Christian times the dance still found some place in the ceremonial of worship.

INTRODUCTION iii

Sir Hubert Parry, in a chapter on dance rhythm in Grove's *Dictionary of Music*, says:—"Dance rhythm and dance gestures have exerted the most powerful influence on music from prehistoric times until to-day. The analogy of a similar state of things among uncultivated races still existing confirms the inherent probability of the view that definiteness of any kind of music, whether of figure or phrase, was first arrived at through connection with dancing. The beating of some kind of noisy instrument as an accompaniment to gestures in the excitement of actual war or victory or other such exciting cause was the first type of rhythmic music, and the telling of tribal or national stories, of deeds of heroes in the indefinite chant consisting of a monotone slightly varying with occasional cadences which is met with among so many barbarous peoples, was the first type of vocal music.

"This vague approach to musical recitation must have received its first rhythmic arrangement when it came to be accompanied by rhythmic gestures and the two processes were thereby combined, while song and dance went on together as in mediæval times in Europe.

"In Oratorio the importance of dance rhythm is shown by negative as well as positive evidence. In the parts in which composers arrived at pure declamatory music, the result, though often expressive, is hopelessly and inextricably indefinite in form. But in most cases they submitted either openly or covertly to dance rhythm in some part or other of their works.

"In Oratorio the dance influence maintained its place, but not so openly as in Opera."

In actual Church worship we find that rhythmic ball was played by bishop and priests round the altar, and at the present day on Corpus Christi Day and other festivals in the Cathedral at Seville the choir boys perform a dance.

The fact that to-day the Christian Festival of Whitsuntide is the most usual time for Morris dancing in those places where it still survives is also an indication that the pagan ceremonial dance was transferred to the Christian Church ceremonial in early Christian times.

Several Churchwarden accounts giving items paid for Morris dancers' clothes, decorations, and regalia also point the same way. One at Kingston-on-Thames reads thus—

		£	s	d
1508. For payneing of the Mores garments and for sarten gret leveres		0	2	4
,, For plyts and ¼ of laun for the Mores garments		0	2	11
,, For Orsden for the same .		0	0	10
,, For bellys for the daunsars		0	0	12

INTRODUCTION

1509-10. For silver paper for the Mores daunsars the frere, and Mayde Maryan at 1d. a peyne	£0	5	4
1521-22. Eight yards of fustyan for the Mores daunsars' coats	0	16	0
,, A dozyn of gold skynnes for the Mores	0	0	10
1536-37. Five hats and 4 poises for the daunsars	0	0	4½

But a carol collected in 1833 from a peasant in West Cornwall and included in William Sandys' collection is the most interesting proof I have yet found of the association between dancing and the Christian religion. Nothing more is known of the Carol in spite of many inquiries which are still being pursued. This is the carol—

TO-MORROW SHALL BE MY DANCING DAY

To-mor-row shall be my danc-ing day, I would my true love did so chance To see the le-gend of my play, To call my true love

114   ENGLISH FOLK-DANCE

to my dance. Sing, oh! my love, Oh, my love, my love, my love, This have I done for my true love.

2. " Then was I born of a Virgin pure,
    Of her I took fleshly substance :
   Then was I knit to man's nature,
    To call my true love to my dance.
        Sing oh! etc.

3. " In a manger laid and wrapp'd I was,
    So very poor this was my chance,
   Betwixt an ox and a silly poor ass,
    To call my true love to my dance.
        Sing oh! etc.

4. " Then afterwards baptised I was,
    The Holy Ghost on me did glance,
   My Father's voice heard from above,
    To call my true love to my dance.
        Sing oh! etc.

5. " Into the desert I was led,
    Where I fasted without substance :
   The Devil bade me make stones my bread,
    To have me break my true love's dance.
        Sing oh! etc.

INTRODUCTION

6. "The Jews on me they made great suit,
    And with me made great variance,
   Because they loved darkness rather than light,
    To call my true love to the dance.
        Sing oh! etc.

7. "For thirty pence Judas me sold,
    His covetousness for to advance;
   Mark, where I kiss, the same do hold,
    The same is he shall lead the dance,
        Sing oh! etc.

8. "Before Pilate the Jews me brought,
    When Barabbas had deliverance;
   They scourg'd me and set me at nought,
    Judged me to die to lead the dance.
        Sing oh! etc.

9. "When on the cross hanged I was;
    When a spear to my heart did glance,
   There issued forth both water and blood,
    To call my true love to the dance.
        Sing oh! etc.

10. "Then down to Hell I took my way,
     For my true love's deliverance,
    And rose again on the third day,
     Up to my true love and the dance.
        Sing oh! etc.

11. "Then up to Heaven I did ascend,
     Where now I dwell in sure substance,
    On the right hand of God, that man
     May come into the general dance.
        Sing oh! etc."

116 ENGLISH FOLK-DANCE

Mr G. R. S. Mead thinks that this carol was originally sung by the mediæval minstrels, jongleurs, and troubadours, who are said to have invented the word carol, meaning a dance in which the performers moved slowly in a circle, singing as they went. The Troubadours are responsible for the preservation of many fragments of old mystery plays, and this carol is probably one such fragment, and as such is a link between the definitely pagan folk-dance and through the Christian Church to those alive in England to-day.

The following tune is taken from Miss A. G. Gilchrist's Manuscript Collection, and was noted and sent to her by Mr Smith Williamson, bandmaster of Moston, W. Manchester, in 1907. Miss Gilchrist thinks it interesting in connection with the tune of this Carol, as it is called "My love, my love," and was played as a Morris dance at the Rush-Cart ceremony at Moston up to forty-five or fifty years ago.

MOSTON RUSH-CART MORRIS TUNE,
"MY LOVE, MY LOVE"

INTRODUCTION

The following account of the sacred all-night dance written by Philo (about A.D. 26) is quoted by Mr Mead in *Quest*, October 1910, and is interesting because the dance described is curiously like the surviving processional dances which have intervals in the processional when a set dance is performed.

"After the banquet they kept the sacred all-night festival. And this is how they keep it. They all stand up in a body, and in the middle of the banqueting-place they first form the Choroi, one of men and the other of women, and a leader and conductor is chosen for each, the one whose reputation is greatest for a knowledge of music: they then chant hymns composed in God's honour in many metres and melodies, sometimes singing together, sometimes one chorus beating the measure with their hands for the antiphonal chanting of the other, now dancing to the measure and now inspiring it, at times dancing in procession, at times set dances, and then circle-dances right and left." The latter part of this description might almost have been taken down from some of the Morris dances danced to-day.

In Anglo-Saxon times the sword dance was in

great repute, and Saxon nobles kept dancers to amuse their guests. There is mention of Morris dancing in Edward III.'s reign, when John of Gaunt returned from Spain, but few, if any, vestiges of it can be traced in writers beyond the reign of Henry VII.: about which time, and particularly in that of Henry VIII., the Churchwarden's accounts in several parishes show that the Morris dance made a very considerable figure in the parochial festivals. Some of the accounts of the May Games of Robin Hood include a Morris dance, but it is doubtful if the Morris was an intrinsic part of the Robin Hood pageant, as it was very often danced on separate occasions altogether. I am inclined to think that both are fragments of much older dances and dramas, and that it is almost impossible to say what was their exact relation to one another. By the time of Henry VIII. and Elizabeth, when references to the Morris dance are very frequent, all idea of its religious significance had disappeared, and it represented the characteristics of the English peasant in a holiday mood in the days when life was a big adventure, and revelry and sport were rude and boisterous. It is a little difficult to realise, as one watches the few remaining traditional dancers to-day, either that their dancing has represented all that mankind knew of primitive religious aspira-

INTRODUCTION

tion and ceremonial, or later that it embodied all the frolic and revel of the rollicking days of Queen Elizabeth.

Although there is only one written record of steps and figures, there are so many general descriptions of the dances in the writers of that time that it is a little difficult, in the short space at my disposal, to choose which will give the best idea of the dance as then performed. I have chosen a few descriptions which seem best to fulfil this purpose.

But first there are four pictures of Morris dancing which may be here described.

The first is a painted glass window at Betley, in Staffordshire. It exhibits in all probability the most curious as well as the oldest representation of an English May game and Morris dance that is anywhere to be found. The dresses look as if they belong to the reign of Edward IV., but the owner, Tollet, thought they were in the time of Henry VIII.

Another early representation of a Morris dance is a copy of a very scarce engraving on copper by Israhel Van Meckenem (died 1503), so named from the place of his nativity, a German village in the confines of Flanders, in which latter country this artist appears chiefly to have resided, and therefore in most of his prints we may observe the Flemish costume of his time. From the pointed shoes that we see in one of the figures it must have been executed between the years 1460 and 1470, about which latter period the broad-toed shoes came into fashion in France and Flanders. It seems to have been intended as a pattern for goldsmith's work, probably a cup or tankard.

And thirdly, there is in the old Town Hall at Munich a series of ten figures of Morris dancers, carved in wood by Erasmus Schnitznar in 1480. All these figures have bells, and one has long streamers to his sleeves.

There is a fourth described by Walpole in his *Catalogue of English Engravers*, under the name of Peter Stent. It is a painting at Lord Fitzwilliam's on Richmond Green, which came out of the old neighbouring palace. It was executed by Vinckenkroom about the end of the reign of James I., and exhibits a view of the above palace. A Morris dance is introduced, consisting of seven figures, viz. :—A fool, hobby horse, piper, Maid Marian, and three dancers, the rest of the figures being spectators.

In a tract entitled *Plaine Percevall the Peace Maker of England*, 1590, mention is made of a " stranger, which, seeing a quintessence (besides the Foole and Maid Marian) of all the picked youth strained out of a whole endship, footing the Morris about a May-pole, and he, not hearing and loving *Bessies*, for bussing them in the darke. Thus all things set in order, then have they their hobby horses, their dragons and other antiques together with their baudie pipers and thundering drummers, to strike up the *Devil's Daunce*, withall: then martch this heathen company towards the Church and Church-yarde, their pypers pyping, their drummers thundering, their stumpes daucing, their belles iyngling, their handkercheefes fluttering about their heades like madde men, their hobbie horses and other monsters skirmishing amongst the throng: and in this sorte they goe to the Church (though the Minister be at prayer or preaching), dauncing and swinging their handkercheefes over their heads in the Church like Devils incarnate, with such a confused noise, that no man can heare his owne voyce."

To come to later times; in a curious story of a Country Squire who turned Methodist and went about the country preaching, called "The Spiritual Quixote or the Summer's Ramble" of Mr Geoffry Wildgoose, a comic romance (1773), there is an amusing account of a Morris dance.

"In the afternoon when they were got within a few miles of Gloucester at a genteel house near the end of the village they saw almost the whole parish assembled in the Court to see a set of Morrice dancers who (this holiday time), dressed

INTRODUCTION

the ministrelsie for the noise of the tabors, bluntly demanded if they were not all beside themselves that they so lip'd and skip'd without an occasion."

Stubbes, in his *Anatomie of Abuses*, thus describes a Morris dance under the title of the "Devil's Daunce."

Description of the Lord of Misrule, and attendant Morris

"First, all the wilde heads of the parish, flocking together, chuse them a graund Captaine (of Mischiefe) whome they innoble with the title of *my Lord of Misrule*, and him they crowne with great solemnitie, and adopt for their King. This king annoynted, chooseth forth twentie, fourtie, three score or a hundred lustie guttes like to himselfe to wait upon his Lordly Majesty, and to guard his noble person. Then everyone of these his men he investeth with his liveries of greene, yellow, or some other light wanton colour. And as though that were not (bawdy) gawdy ynough, I should say, they bedecke themselves with scarffes, ribbons and laces hanged all over with golde ringes, precious stones and other jewels: this done, they tie about either legge twentie or fourtie belles with rich handkerchiefe in their handes and sometimes laide a cross over their shoulders and neckes, borrowed for the most part of their pretie *Mopsies*

Morris Dancers in the time of James I.

up in bells and ribbands, were performing for the entertainment of the family of some company that had dined there.

. . . . .

"Those who are acquainted with this sort of Morrice dance (which is still practised in several parts of England) must know that they are usually attended with one character called the Tom fool, who like the clown in the pantomime seems to be a burlesque upon all the rest. His fool's cap has a fox's tail depending like a ramillie whip: and instead of the small bells which the others wear on their legs he has a great sheep-bell hung on his back side. Whilst the company therefore were all attention to the preacher this buffoon contrived to slip the fool's cap upon Tugwell's head, and to fix the sheep's bell to his rump. Which Jerry no sooner perceived than his choler arose, and spitting into his hands and clenching his fists he gave the Tom fool a swinging blow in the face. Tugwell pursued with the sheep bell at his tail. Ended the preaching."

At Abingdon-on-Thames the date on the regalia of the Morris dances still in existence is 1700, and the Bampton Morris "side" claims an unbroken tradition, so that in these places at any rate we are in touch with the dance as it has come to us from the days when it was an inherent part of country life, and it is from these and other isolated "sides" and individuals that the steps, figures, and tunes have been taken down at the present day. A complete reconstruction of the dance is of course impossible, so is an exact lesson of the way in which it should be danced, but with the general descriptions and the remaining dancers enough can be ascertained to justify the contention that England has a real folk-dance of her own which compares very favourably with that of other nations.

ORCHESOGRAPHIE

mes Asdicnsi, lors voulu dancer auec des marque pieds, & marque talons mestez cy ensemble. L'exercice de tout cela te rois forcer, si ennaturament celle qu'a s par tappements de pieds, a fait congnoistre par experience, que finablement on y engendre la podagre & maladies des gouttes: parquoy cette dance est tombée en desuetude. Ie ne laisseray de vous en donner l'art, auec les mouuements à va passage, & quand aux autres passages, vous les pourrez apprendre de ceux qui y sont stilez, desquels pour le iourd'huy s'en treuue bien petit nombre.

Tabulature des Morisques.

Air de Morisques.

Mouuements.
frappe talon droit. Le bouc en de Morisques tient frappe talon gauche. le bout des ortels toujours fer- frappe talon droit. me, ne descendant que la frappe des frappe talon gauche talons, puis faire reformer sa frappe talons. sommeraise, & la frappe talon soupir. fans dansse deux ou quatre- frappe talon droit. geoissent pas de multi. frappe talon gauche. frappe talon droit. frappe talon gauche. frappe talons. soupir. frappe talon droit. frappe talon gauche. frappe talon droit. frappe talon gauche.

DE THOINOT ARBEAU.

Continuation de l'air de Morisque, comme aussi du mouuement.

frappe talon droit.
frappe talon gauche.
frappe talon droit.
frappe talon gauche.
frappe talon droit.
frappe talon gauche.
frappe talon droit.
frappe talon gauche.
frappe talons.
soupir.

Capriol.

Ainsi que on deduisez les mouuements de cette Morisque, il semble que le danceur ne bougera d'une place.

Arbeau.

Il fault bien qu'il marche tousiours auant, iusques au bout de la sale. Et pour ce faire, notterez qu'aprez le frappe talons qui equipolle a pied sous & cadance, auant le frappe talon droit, il aduiendra une legere remise à deux pieds, & ce pendant cela se fait, les dits frappe talons droits. Car il vous considererez bien, apres les pieds ioincts, le frappe talon droit soyt. Notterez aussi, que ce fust air de Morisques se doibt oupper per ostrouher, & a chacune d'icelles, faict des frappe talons comme dessus.

I. THE MORRIS DANCE TO-DAY

BEFORE the revival of Morris dancing in 1905, there was only one description of the steps and evolutions of the dance, and that was in *Orchesographie et Traicte en Forme de Dialogue*, by Thoinot Arbeau, published in 1588.

This is so interesting that I have had a photograph of it taken from the copy in the British Museum.

The Morris dance may be roughly divided into five kinds — processional, corner, handkerchief, stick dances, and solo jigs.

The corner dances are danced with handkerchiefs and so are the processional and jigs, but there are also others where handkerchiefs take the place of sticks.

Since 1905 Mr Cecil Sharp has published instructions for the Morris dance in a series called the Morris Book, with the tunes as played at the present day. The first two volumes of the series were written in collaboration with Mr H. C. MacIlwaine, and with the help of Miss Florence Warren, of the Espérance Guild of Morris dancers, from whom the steps of most of the dances were

126 ENGLISH FOLK-DANCE

taken down as she had learned them from William Kimber, of Headington.

I have also edited, with the help of Mr Clive Carey, Mr Geoffrey Toye, and Miss Florence Warren, two volumes called *The Espérance Morris Book*, and Mr John Graham has collected Midland, Lancashire, and Cheshire dances in two volumes.[1]

It is probable that these books contain complete instructions in the steps and figures of the dance and are a fairly complete collection of the existing dances, and that others still in the Collector's books, but not yet published, may only be variants. There is a varied and extensive terminology used by the old dancers, and it is often difficult to arrive at the exact meaning of certain expressions, for each set of dancers has its own phraseology, which varies considerably from that of other sets even when they are not many miles apart in locality. The following are some of the terms used:—"Shake up" and "foot up" for the first figure of a dance; "hey up" or "hey sides up," "back to back," "hands across," and "capers." "Gipsies" must be seen to be understood, and "galley" is a turning round on your own axis with a single or double shake of the leg, which

[1] Both the first volume of *The Espérance Morris Book* and the first volume of Mr Sharp's *Morris Book* have been revised.

THE MORRIS DANCE TO-DAY

seems to be better done the older and more shaky the dancer is.

Each village has its own steps and its own evolutions, and the evolutions generally follow the same order in each dance, the particular steps of that dance being done between the evolutions.

This is a very usual order in which the dance is done—

Foot up or Shake up.
Special step.
Hey up.
Special step.
Hands across.
Special step.
Back to back.
Special step.
Hey up and All in.

But it would take a whole volume to describe each step done by each "side" of dancers, and by the time this book was in print other variants would have arisen, if any of the "sides" had danced in the meantime.

For practical purposes one has to decide on the most typical step one has seen and adopt it for those to whom one is responsible for teaching the dances.

But the characteristics of all the dances are vigour and virility, and there is nothing in the least like the posturing with pointed toe which characterises the ordinary ball-room and stage dances.

ENGLISH FOLK-DANCE

The following is a complete list as far as I know of all the Morris dances collected and published since the revival in 1905:—

- Bean-setting.
- Laudnum Bunches.
- Country Gardens.
- Constant Billy.
- Trunkles.
- Rigs o' Marlow.
- Bluff King Hal.
- How d'ye do, Sir?
- Shepherds' Hey.
- Blue-eyed Stranger.
- Hey diddle Dis.
- Hunting the Squirrel.
- Getting up Stairs.
- Double set Back.
- Haste to the Wedding.
- Rodney.
- Processional Morris.
- Jockie to the Fair.
- Old Mother Oxford.
- Old Woman tossed up in a blanket.
- Bacca Pipes jig.
- Flowers of Edinburgh.
- The Rose.
- Field Town Morris.
- The Maid of the Mill.
- Bobbing Joe.
- Glorisheers.
- The Gallant Hussar
- Leap Frog.
- Shooting.
- Brighton Camp.
- Green Garters.
- Princess Royal.
- Lumps of Plum Pudding.
- The Fool's Dance.
- Derbyshire Morris.
- Derbyshire Morris Reel.
- The Cuckoo's Nest.
- The Monk's March.
- Longborough Morris.
- Heel and Toe.
- Bobby's Joan.
- Banks of the Dee.
- Dearest Dicky.
- London Pride.
- Swaggering Boney.
- Young Collins.
- All's for the Best and Richmond Hill.

THE MORRIS DANCE TO-DAY

Step Back.[1]
I'll go and enlist for a Sailor.
Sherborne Jig.
None so Pretty.
Cross Caper, or Prince's Royal.
We won't go home till Morning.
Abraham Brown.
Morris Off.
Long Morris.
Cross Morris.
Three Cans Morris.
Nancy Dawson.
The Boatman's Song.
The Tight Little Island.
The Girl I left behind Me.
The Rose Tree and The British Grenadiers.
Garryowen.
With a Hundred Pipers.
Ninety-five.
Draw Back.
Bumpus o' Stretton.
Lively Jig.
Morris On.
Sally Luker.
A Nutting we will go.

In addition to these Mr F. Kidson has also published a set of Country and Morris dance tunes, but without instructions as to the dances.

Although this list gives a very fair idea of the traditional Morris dances still lingering in country places, two things must be borne in mind—first, that many of these dances with different names

[1] As far as I can gather, this is the dance called "Molly Oxford" by the Field Town dancers; it seems that Mr Sharp has substituted this name owing to the fact that it is not danced to the "Molly Oxford" tune. One of the dancers repudiates the title on the ground that the characteristic figure is a spring and not a step back.

are practically the same dances; another tune and a very slight alteration in the step is quite enough for a Morris dancer to say he has another dance to show; and secondly, that the collectors have not yet finished their work. I have in my possession quite a long list of people and places as yet unvisited which may yield dances yet unrecorded, and Mr Cecil Sharp has announced many dances and variants collected but not published.

The Folk-dance has been found in the following counties:—

Gloucestershire.	Monmouthshire.
Oxfordshire.	Yorkshire.
Berkshire.	Lancashire.
Northamptonshire.	Cheshire.
Lincolnshire.	Northumberland.
Derbyshire.	Warwickshire.
Nottinghamshire.	Worcestershire.
Sussex.	Surrey.
Cornwall.	

II. TUNES

A word must be said about the tunes played for the dances by country musicians to-day.

These tunes are, of course, of much later date than the Morris and Sword dances, and probably contemporary with the original country dances.

TUNES

The musicians took any tune which was popular at the time and adapted it to the dances, so that the tunes are not by any means all traditional. As an instance of this, I remember that old Mr Trafford, of Headington, told me that one day when he heard a military band playing, he went and listened at the door of the barracks, and that he was so attracted by the tune that he at once hummed it to the Morris dance fiddler and adapted it to a Morris dance. To this day he likes the tune, which he calls "Buffalo Gals,"[1] so much that he wanted Mr Carey to take it down and use it. There is no doubt that at any given time the musicians used to adapt to the dances any popular tune that took their fancy, and I think that probably the name of the dance was altered to fit the tune. Anyway the tune which Mr Trafford liked, called "The Buffalo Girls," had certainly been taken for the name of a dance. The only dance tune that I have been able to discover which has its dance steps attached to it is the one before mentioned in Arbeau's book. There is no doubt either that the nature of the tunes changed considerably as the whittle and dub went out of fashion and were superseded by the fiddle and later by the concertina, from which latter instrument the first revived tunes

[1] A Christy minstrel tune, popular some years back.

were taken by Mr Sharp from William Kimber. The tunes taken from the violin were more likely to be played in a modal scale; for instance, Kimber played "The Rigs of Marlow" in the modern scale, but Mark Cox, who gave it to us from the fiddle, played it in a modal form.

In the summer of 1912 the fiddler who played for the Morris dancers at "Shakspeare's England" in a few days played in a modal form a tune which had been given him in the modern scale and was quite unconscious that he had altered it.

Two Morris dance tunes, "Bean-setting" and "Laudnum Bunches," do not seem to be allied to any other forms of the airs.

In insisting on the traditional nature of the dances it is necessary to admit that the same cannot be said of all, or even most, of the tunes played to-day.

III. MUSICAL INSTRUMENTS

IN the earliest records of Morris dancing, the pipe and tabor, or whittle and dub, were the musical instruments in use, and the oldest dancers to-day are never tired of lamenting that the pipe and tabor to which they danced in their youth have gone out of fashion.

A Morris dancer in Fleet Street, London, is

MUSICAL INSTRUMENTS

described in a seventeenth century manuscript in the British Museum (Harleian MS. 3910):

> "In Fleet Strete then I heard a shoote:
> I putt of my hatt, and I made no staye,
> And when I came unto the roote,
> Good Lord ! I heard a taber play,
> For so, God save me, a morrys-daunce."

In the old play of *Jacke Drums Entertainment* (1601)—

The taber and pipe strike up a morrice.
A shoute within.
Ed. Oh, a moirice is come, observe our country sports,
'Tis Whitsun-tyde and we must frolick it.

Enter the Morrice.

THE SONG

Skip it and trip it, nimbly, nimbly,
Tickle it, tickle it lustily,
Strike up the taber, for the wenches favour,
Tickle it, tickle it lustily.

Let us be seen in Hygate Greene,
To dance for the honour of Holloway.
Since we are come hither, let's spare no leather,
To dance for the honour of Holloway."

Later the fiddle took the place of pipe and tabor, and still more recently the concertina.

The present-day fiddler at Bampton, Mr Wells, and Mr Mark Cox of Headington are well worth a visit from musicians interested in the actual form in which the tunes are played to-day by the musically unlettered.

Mr William Kimber, jun., of Headington, is also in possession of the old tunes, which he plays skilfully on the concertina. Patience will be needed should the tunes be noted, for very few musicians can repeat a phrase, even if it is the very last bar, without going right back to the beginning of the tune. When the phrase is intricate, and has to be often repeated, this means that a considerable amount of time is taken up. The same applies to the dance; the traditional dancer is quite unselfconscious, and if he is pulled up and asked for a repetition of a step, he cannot give it, as a rule, without going back to the beginning of the dance; so that in writing down the steps and evolutions of the dance much patience is needed and understanding of the way in which the minds of simple folk work.

Within the memory of some of the oldest dancers the dancing was always accompanied by singing, and old Master Druce, of Ducklington, told us that the Morris could not be properly danced without singing. He could, however, only remember a few of the words of one dance—"The Lollypop Man."

The Bampton men gave us a few odd verses of

MUSICAL INSTRUMENTS

one or two songs, but I am afraid the real song will never be recovered, for, as one old man put it to a friend of mine, "the words are too clumsy for girls."

Miss Gilchrist gave me the words of a Lancashire Morris which we have often used with very good effect—

> "Morris dance is a very pretty tune,
> Lads and lassies plenty,
> Every lad shall have his lass,
> And I'll have four and twenty.
>
> My new shoone they are so good,
> I could dance Morris if I would,
> And if hat and coat be dressed,
> I will dance Morris with the best.
>
> This is it and that is it,
> And this is Morris dancing,
> My poor father broke his leg,
> And so it was a'chancing.
>
> Bread and cheese and the old cow's head
> Roasted in a lantern,
> A bit for me and a bit for you,
> And a bit for the Morris dancer."

Even in this doggerel there are traces of the old sacrificial rite of animal sacrifice in which the head was considered as the most sacred part of the animal and much coveted. It was generally awarded to the victor or victorious side in a fight for its possession.

IV. THE DRESS

THE Morris dance dress had two characteristics; it was the holiday attire of the dancers and it had added to that certain special ceremonial features. These were bells, ribbons, sticks or swords, and handkerchiefs.

In the Kingston-on-Thames Churchwardens' Accounts (1536-37) the dresses of the Morris dancers are thus described:—They consisted of four coats of white fustian spangled, and two green satin coats with garters on which small bells were fastened. In an old tract called "Old Meg of Herefordshire for a Mayde Marian, and Hereford Town for a Morris Daunce" (1609), the musicians and the twelve dancers have "long coats of the old fashion, high sleeves gathered at the elbows, and hanging sleeves behind: the stuff red buffin striped with white, girdles with white stockings, white and red roses to their shoes: the one Six, a white jew's cap with a jewel and a long red feather: the other a scarlet jew's cap with a jewel and a white feather." Scarves, ribbands, and laces hung all over with gold rings, and even precious stones are also mentioned in the time of Elizabeth. Miles, the Miller of Ruddington, in Sampson's

THE DRESS

play, " The Vow Breaker, or the Fayre Maid of Clifton" (1636), says he is come to borrow "a few ribbands, bracelets, eare-rings, wyasyters and silke girdle and hand-kerchers for a morris."

Joe Miller, writing in 1874, gives the following description of the preparations of a Morris dance :—
" One Molly o' Cheetham's sent specially to London for bows and flowerets to dress her Robin's hat with, and Jenny of the Warden House Cottage kept her thumb nail strapped up for a month to crimp her Billy's ruffled shirt. She was so feared of spoiling the edge of the nail : and Phœbe of the Dean Farm, took Billy's breeches to St Ann's Square (Manchester) to have them laced with blue ribbons and bows down the side. All the lasses of the village were as busy as bees, making bows, getting up fine shirts, and tying white handkerchiefs with ribbons to dance with."

The late Mr Alfred Burton, writing in 1891, says :—" The costume worn now and for many years past (colour being left to individual taste, except in the case of the breeches, which are generally of the same colour and material in each band of dancers) consists of shoes with buckles, white stockings, knee breeches tied with ribbons, a brightly coloured scarf or sash round the waist, white shirt trimmed with ribbons and fastened with brooches, and white straw hats decorated with ribbons and rosettes. White handkerchiefs or streamers are tied to the wrist."

Strutt, in his *Sports and Pastimes of the People of England* (1810), observes that the garments of the Morris dancers were adorned with bells, which were not placed there merely for the sake of ornament, but were to be sounded as they danced. These bells were of unequal sizes and differently denominated, as the fore-bell, the second-bell, the treble, and the tenor or great bell, and mention is also made of double bells. Sometimes they used trebles only, but these refinements were of later times. At first, these bells were small and numerous and affixed to all parts of the body—the neck, shoulders, elbows, wrists, waist, knee, and ankle : the wrist, knee, and ankle being, however, the principal places. The number of bells round each leg sometimes amounted to from twenty to forty. They were occasionally jingled by the hands.

The following description of a Morris dancer taken from *Recreations for Ingenious Head Pieces* (1667) gives a very good idea of his appearance at that date :—

> "With a noyse and a din,
> Comes the Maurice dancer in,
> With a fine linnen shirt, but a buckram skin.
>   Oh ! he treads out such a peale,
>   From his paire of legs of veale.

> The quarters are idols to him.
> Nor do those knaves inviron
> Their toes with so much iron,
> 'Twill ruin a smith to shoe him."

The Morris dancers' dress has fallen on somewhat evil days of late years. The best they can do is a white suit of duck or flannel with trousers, short knee breeches, or even ordinary dark cloth trousers with a white shirt. The shirt is decorated with ribbons and rosettes, and sometimes a double baldric is worn crossed on the chest and hanging down at the sides. The bells are sewn on to a pad, and a pair which I have is made of long bits of coloured cloth such as a sailor uses to make a hearthrug with, the bells sewn in between. This was got from a pawnshop in Oxford with a pipe and tabor, a pathetic sign of the decay of national gaiety!

The hat is sometimes a box hat, sometimes a bowler, sometimes a cap, but it must be gaily decorated with ribbons and artificial flowers, bits of feather, or anything that comes in handy. Mr Brookes, of Godley Hill, who came to London to teach the Lancashire dances, wore a bowler hat covered tightly with white calico, and over that a mass of flowers, and ribbons hanging down behind.

I confess that this curious mixture of a traditional ceremonial dress and the modern bowler hat does not attract me nor appeal to my sense of the fitness of things, but I think that for present-day performance one must either adopt the least objectionable form of present-day holiday dress, which is usually white flannel, add as much colour as possible in ribbons and sash, and leave it at that, or if any fancy dress is adopted I think it is best to adopt the Elizabethan peasants' holiday dress and add the bells, ribbons, etc., as it was during her reign that the Morris dance was very usually danced at fairs and festivals.

The only woman's dress described in old writers is that of Maid Marian, but as the character was taken by a man dressed as a woman, who was very grotesquely dressed, it is better to-day to adopt a very simple dress, such as a cotton frock and a sun bonnet, with a bunch of ribbons at the waist. Every girl should have a different colour, though the general style may be the same.

The shoes of the dancers should be ordinary walking shoes with low heels and no pointed toes, because these dances were danced in the open air and on the open road. A good dancer can make the "bells speak" even on a boarded floor, and that is all that is necessary. I think that any sort of thin ballet shoe is quite out of place and spoils the character of an open-air dance.

V. EXTRA CHARACTERS

In the days when the Morris dance was an integral part of the people's life it was no one's business to make exact records in writing either of the dance itself, of the ceremonies connected with it, or of the characters associated with it. It is therefore very difficult to differentiate with any exactitude just where the Morris dance merged into the sword dance, and just where the dances were merged into the Mummers' plays and other early pageants and ceremonies.

All primitive forms of dance and drama are attempts to express man's worship of the natural forces and facts of life, so that we shall expect to find other characters than those of the actual dancers. The most common of these are the Lord and Lady, the King and Queen, evidently representing early ideas of the masculine and feminine principles in nature and worshipped as the forces which brought the return of the green life of spring to the earth. Both these characters also occur separately in some places, the King being called Mayor, a Lord of Misrule, a very curious survival of the Mock King of Saturnalian revels, who after a short reign of feasting and festivity is sacrificed that a new king may reign in his stead.

One very old man whom I met, and who shall remain unnamed and unlocated, boasted to me that he had been this Mayor of the Morris nine times. The qualification for this honour, I learned elsewhere in the town, was to have been locked up three times in one year for being drunk and three times in one year for beating your wife! In emphasising the religious origin of these dances it is well to bear in mind that the religion they express is not precisely that of the orderly Church and Chapel-going folk of to-day, and that no sort of gloom or depression was allowed to mar the joy of the ceremonial, even when the end of the principal actor was known to be execution at the point of the sword. As Dr Frazer remarks, "in these circumstances it was natural that the principal actor should be recruited from the gaol more often than from the green-room."

The Queen was also called the Moll, Maid Marian, the Lady of the Lamb, Bessie, and The Lady of the May, and was a man, generally a smooth-faced youth, who was dressed as and represented a woman.

A very important character was the Fool, Tom Fool, Dysard, Squire, or Rodney, identical with the jongleur or joculator. He was often the best dancer, did special feats to amuse the crowd, and

EXTRA CHARACTERS

with a cow's tail and bladder attached to the ends of a stick kept the crowd from encroaching on the dancers. The Fool survived in Lancashire as "owd Sooty face," "Dirty Bet," and "owd Molly Coddle" as late as 1891.

The Hobby-Horse was a great feature of the dance in early days. Its wild capering and frolicking around added much to the general amusement. Mr Cecil Sharp says that he has not met with a traditional dancer who remembers a hobby horse being part of the Morris side, but there are numerous allusions to it in writing.

In "Cobbe's Prophecies, his Signs and Tokens, his Madrigalls, Questions and Answers" (1614), the following occurs:—

> "And fine Maide Marian with her smoile,
> Shew'd how a rascall plaide the roile:
> But, when the Hobby-Horse did wihy,
> Then all the wenches gave a tihy."

Robin Hood and Friar Tuck also appear occasionally in historic accounts, but I have never heard of either character as part of the "sides" now existing.

The musician, once a player on pipe and tabor, later on the fiddle, and to-day sometimes on the concertina, was of course indispensable, and I was told at Headington of one old fiddler for that "side," who played until he was so old that he had to be carried from place to place and deposited on the roadside when the dancers halted for the dance, and I heard of another who rode a donkey when too old to accompany the dancers on foot.

The Treasurer who carried the collecting box is also important. Most "sides" of Morris men had a "sword-bearer," who carried round a gaily-decorated sword on which was impaled a cake, specially made for the occasion by some lady who undertook the duty year by year, though of late (as at Bampton) the cake is just an ordinary shop-made one. A small knife is stuck in the cake, and the sword-bearer hands it round to the spectators, who each ceremonially take a piece. The "treasurer" follows with a box into which one is expected to put a donation to compensate the dancers "for their trouble."

The effect of the ceremony is quite extraordinary. To go from the London of to-day to a quiet village and take part in this old ritual is to know the link which binds the ornate Catholic ritual of to-day to the most primitive ritual evolved by the folk to express the truths of incarnation, of sacrifice, of death, and of resurrection. To go from Kirtlington, where in the traditional tales of the oldest inhabitants there are still traces of the

Whit Monday at Bampton-in-the-Bush, Oxon.

THE SWORD DANCE

human sacrifice, and later of a lamb sacrificed as a substitute, and to go on to Bampton, where the cake alone typifies the ancient sacrificial rite, is to realise the power inherent in the human race to lay aside in each generation some cruelty, some horror, and to rise by slow degrees into a higher state of evolution. The study of folk-dance and of the legend and ceremonial which surround it opens up a great field of interest to all who would learn the secrets of human development.

VI. THE SWORD DANCE

THE Sword dance is still performed in the North of England, generally at Christmas time and on Plough Monday, 6th of January. It was originally part of a pageant or Mummers' play in which the ever-recurring drama of death and resurrection was acted in various forms.

Mr Sharp says that traces of it have been found in two southern English counties. Mr Carey found a dance called " Over the Sticks " in Sussex, but it has more of the characteristics of the Scotch sword dance, in which the swords are placed on the ground and the dancer shows his skill by dancing elaborate steps over and between the swords.

Sometimes in the Midlands a similar dance is found in which long Churchwarden pipes take the place of the sticks. The sword dances of Northern England are quite different, and are allied to those found in many European countries. These show traces of ancient ceremonial worship and the slaying of the sacrificial victim, and are more in the nature of drama than dance.

In *Mysterium und Mimus im Rigveda*, by Leopold von Schroeder (1908), there are some very interesting suggestions as to the meaning of these ceremonial sword dances, one of which, referring to the sword dance of Yorkshire called the Giants' dance, runs as follows (p. 118):—"The leading feature of the dance, which was performed by masked peasants, was that two swords were swung around and on to the neck of a boy without hurting him. The circumstance is of great importance that the leading giant was called Woden and his wife Frigg. This shows us the mythological significance of the dance, clearly and without doubt. Whilst we here see Woden stepping forth as a great dancer, as the chief of a troop of giant dancers, we get a new and important feature in the representation of the god which makes him still more like the wild dancer Rudra-Shiva, a feature of which we hear nothing from other accounts of Wodan-Odin, and yet which is

THE SWORD DANCE

undoubtedly old and real. We must picture to ourselves here not the great heavenly god of the Edda, but rather the still far more primitive though already powerful spirit of the wind, of the soul, and of fruitfulness, from which the great god Woden has developed. Perhaps, too, we may see in the boy round whose neck the sword was swung harmlessly, the new-born, youthful spirit of fruitfulness: whom the swords shall symbolically protect, whose growth and thriving the sword dance, as a magical enchantment bearing fruitfulness, was in all probability intended to promote. In the same way the Curetes held the sword dance round the young Zeus, and the Corybantes round the infant Dionysos, in order to protect him. In my opinion it was also to promote his growth."

One is not so dependent on present-day dancers for a description of the sword dances as one is for that of the Morris dances, for certain records have survived. Olaus Magnus, in his *History of the Northern Nations*, thus describes the sword dance as practised by the Swedes and Goths:—
"First with their swords sheathed and erect in their hands they dance in a triple round. Then with their drawn swords held erect as before, afterwards extending them from hand to hand, they lay hold of each other's hilt and point while

they are wheeling more moderately round, and changing their order, throw themselves into the figure of a hexagon which they call a rose. But presently, raising and drawing back their swords they undo that figure to form (with them) a four-square rose that may rebound over the head of each. At last they dance rapidly backwards, and vehemently rattling the sides of their swords together conclude the sport. Pipes or songs (sometimes both) direct the measure, which at first is slow, but increasing afterwards becomes a very quick one towards the conclusion."

He calls this a kind of Gymnastic Rite in which the ignorant were successively instructed by those who were skilled in it.

The first sword dance I saw performed was the Earsdon, which was accompanied by the small pipes. It looks very complicated, and is more interesting from an antiquarian point of view than from that of a dance. The performers keep huddled up together, and it is difficult for a spectator to see much of what is going on. The second one I saw was at Flamborough, and it was danced by eight fishermen who have learnt it traditionally for longer than anyone living to-day can tell. This is a much more attractive dance, with more variety in the figures, and is almost identical with the description given by Olaus

Photo by J H Graham

"The Lock"; Characteristic of Sword Dances

THE SWORD-DANCE

Magnus. Eventually I had two of the fishermen up to London, and they taught the dance to eight young men, who have in their turn passed it on to a great many others. Mr Fuller Maitland has published the Sword Dance Song of Kirkby Malzeard in *English County Songs*, with the music. He considers that the tune of the Prologue has much of the Morris dance character, and that it was probably used for the actual dancing. The song describes each of the dancers, who comes out from among the rest as he is described by the singer. Old Thomas Wood of Kirkby Malzeard told Mr Bower, who took down the tune, that he would have nothing to do with the present Christmas sword dancers, or Moowers, "who have never had the full of it, and don't dress properly nor do it in any form, being a bad, idle company." They were originally taught by him, to make up his numbers at the Ripon Millenary Festival.

Mr Sharp has collected seven sword dances, including those of Earsdon, Flamborough, and Kirkby Malzeard, but probably none are danced as they were in the old days before more modern amusements took the place of the old folk festivals.

The sword dance, like the Morris, was essentially a man's dance, and whereas many of the Morris dances are quite suitable for women, the sword dance should be kept strictly as a man's dance.

ENGLISH FOLK-DANCE

VII. THE FURRY DANCE

The Furry dance comes under the heading of a genuine folk dance and is part of an old ritual of May Day. Mrs Lily Grove gives the following account of it:—

"The Fadé or Furry dance takes place in the parish of Helston, on Furry Day, May 8th, which to dwellers in those parts is like Christmas Day to most English people."

Fadé is an old Cornish word meaning "to go," and is often corrupted into faddy, while furry is by some authorities derived from the Cornish fuer, signifying fair or merry-making. Mr Quin, in the *Royal Cornwall Gazette* of May 13th, 1864, gives the following description of the dance:—

"There were forty-one couples. They just trip it on in couples hand in hand, during the first part of the Furry dance tune forming a long string, the gentleman leading his partner with his right hand: second part of the tune, the first gentleman turns with both hands, the lady behind him and her partner turns the same way with the first lady, then each gentleman in the same manner with his own partner; then trip as before, each part of the tune being repeated. The other couples pair and turn the same way and at the same time. The movement is elegant. The party proceed up one side of the street and down the other, passing through all the houses they choose."

This dance is very like the spring dance of other countries, where it was customary to stop before every door to give a blessing and ask for contributions. Any house omitted was considered unlucky. Men and women both take part in this dance, and the alternate processional and figure dancing shows that it is probably of the same nature as the Tideswell processional dance. It is in this respect also like the "Lancashire Morris processional," "Long Morris," and the tune of the Furry dance is like the tune of " Long Morris."

Goosey Dancing.—There is also the Cornish " Goosey Dancing," which is danced by boys and girls, and which has much in common with Saturnalian revels. It is danced at Christmas time for a week, ending on Plough Monday.

The word "goosey" probably comes from " guised," for it is customary to dress up for the festivities and for the boys and girls to change dresses. This is a very usual feature of Saturnalian revels, and much shocked the Puritans, as it is contrary to the express law of Deuteronomy.

The Gienys Dance.—In the Isle of Man, on January 6th, the Gienys Dance is held, and the mainstyr or master of the ceremony appoints every man his tegad or valentine for the year.

The Abbot's Bromley Horn Dance.—Mr Sharp has included this in his book of Sword Dances. The dancers have stags' horns attached to their heads, but there is no very distinctive step.

VIII. THE COUNTRY DANCE

A FEW country dances are still remembered by old people living in villages, but, unlike the Morris dances, by far the greater number of country dances are recorded both as to steps and figures, so that they do not come under the same heading as the strictly traditional dance. The supposition that "country-dance" is a corruption of "contre-danse," and that it came to England from France, is not correct. It was in fact, as in name, a country dance, danced by country folk in barn and ale-house and on village greens. It travelled to France, and was called there the "Contre danse." Later these dances were adopted by the upper classes and even penetrated into Court

THE COUNTRY DANCE 153

circles. At this time they were at their best, and many were danced in the round form, but gradually this form became obsolete, until in the middle of the eighteenth century only the dances "longways for as many as will" were danced.

In Grove's *Dictionary of Music* Mr Kidson gives an account of a dance called "Mall Peatly, the new way," which he has seen danced in a cottage on a Yorkshire moor. "You are to hit your right elbows together and then your left, and turn with your left hands behind and your right hands before, and turn twice round and then your left elbows together, and turn as before and so to the next." Mr Cecil Sharp has collected a number of country dances still danced by country folk, and Mr Clive Carey has also collected country dances, principally in Sussex. But the great mine of wealth wherein are the greatest numbers of these beautiful, old-fashioned dances is *Playford's Dancing Master*.

The first edition of this collection is entitled "The English Dancing Master: or Plain and Easie Rules for the Dancing of Country Dances, with the tune to each dance (104 pages of music). Printed by Thomas Harper, and are to be sold by John Playford at his shop in the Inner Temple neere the Church doore." The date is 1651, but it was entered at Stationers' Hall on the 7th of November, 1650.

The next is "The Dancing Master, . . . second edition, enlarged and corrected from many grosse errors which were in the former edition." This was printed by John Playford in 1652 (112 pages of Music). The two next editions, those of 1657 and 1665, each contain 132 Country Dances, and are counted by Playford as one edition. To both were added the tunes of the most usual French Dances, and also other new and pleasant English Tunes for the Treble Violin. (The tunes for the Violin were afterwards printed separately as "Apollo's Banquet," and are not included in any other edition of the *Dancing Master*.) The date of the fourth edition is 1670 (155 pages of Music). The fifth edition, 1675 (160 pages of Music). The sixth edition, from advertisements in Playford's other publications, appears to have been printed in 1680. The seventh edition bears the date 1686 (208 pages), but to this "an additional sheet," containing thirty-two tunes, was first added, then "a new additional sheet of twelve pages," and lastly "a new addition of six more." The eighth edition was printed by E. Jones for H. Playford, and great changes made in the airs. It has 220 pages, date 1690. The ninth edition, 196 pages, date 1695. The second

THE COUNTRY DANCE

part of the *Dancing Master*, 24 pages, date 1696. The tenth edition, 215 pages, date 1698, also the second edition of the second part, ending on page 48 (irregularly paged), 1698. The eleventh edition, 312 pages, date 1701. The twelfth edition, 354 pages, date 1703.

A sixteenth and a seventeenth edition, which, however, are identical, are in the Bodleian Library.

The directions for the dance were written under each, but only the figures are given, but no steps. The following directions for one of the dances, "All in a Garden Green," will give an idea of the curious phraseology of the book:—

ALL IN A GARDEN GREEN. Longways for six.

Lead up all a D. forwards and back, set and turn S. ∸; that again ∴.

First man shake his own Wo. by the hand, then the 2, then the 3, by one hand, then by the other, kisses her twice and turn her ∸, shake her by the hand, then the 2, then your own by one hand, then by the other, kiss her twice and turn her ∴.

Sides all, set and turn S. ∸; that again ∴. This as before, the We. doing it ∴.

Arms all, set and turn S. ∸; that again ∴. This as before, the men doing it ∴.

ENGLISH FOLK-DANCE

A Table explaining the characters which are set down in the Rules for Dancing

- D. Is for double. A double is four steps forward and backward, closing both feet.
- S. Is for a single. A single is two steps, closing both feet.
- Wo. Stands for Woman.
- We. Stands for Women.
- Cu. Stands for Couple.
- Co. Stands for Contrary.
- 2. Stands for Second.
- 3. Stands for Third.
- 4. Stands for Fourth.
- ∸ This is for a strain play'd once.
- ∺ This is for a strain play'd twice.
  These two characters expresse the figures of the dance.
- ☉ This stands for the Man.
- ☽ This stands for the Woman.

In 1904 Miss Nellie Chaplin gave a performance of dances including the "Pavane," "Galliard," "Allemande," "Courante," "Sarabande," and "Chacone," and in 1906 led, through her study of old instruments and old music, to an interest in other ancient dances, and with the help of an expert in dancing she deciphered several of

THE COUNTRY DANCE 157

the dances from *Playford's Dancing Master*, harmonised the tunes, added the appropriate steps from her collaborator's knowledge of dancing, and began to give public performances of the dances in London and different parts of the country. No one who has ever seen these pupils of hers, with their beautiful, old-fashioned dresses, dancing the old-world dances accompanied by a string quartette and oboe, will ever forget the charm of the performance. Miss Chaplin chose some of the most complicated of the dances for revival, and has made the dancing of them a real art. Some years later, Mr Cecil Sharp published a number of Playford's tunes and dances which were performed by the young ladies of the South-Western Polytechnic, generally as illustrations of his lectures on folk-dancing. They are now given by the Folk-Dance Society at their performances. His method of giving the dances is different from Miss Chaplin's, because his pupils, unlike hers, do not use any steps, but only give the figures with a walking or running step, which is the same in all the dances. Which method is best is purely a matter of taste.

Through Miss Chaplin, the Folk-Dance Society, and the Espérance Guild, the country dances are now once more danced by numbers of people all over the country, and it is to be hoped that they will never again recede between the covers of a dancing-master's book.

The country dance tunes are often ballad tunes.

The tunes played to-day by country fiddlers are often found in early books of opera and printed collections of airs.

For instance, the tune of Tink-a-Tink, a country dance collected by Mr Sharp and published in Set II. of *Country Dance Tunes, collected from Traditional Sources*, is a song in the Opera "Bluebeard," by Michael Kelly, published in 1799.

"The Butterfly" in Set I. of the same series is apparently a remembrance of the once popular "I'd be a Butterfly," the words and melody by Thomas Haynes Bayly. It is included in many books of airs.

The tunes did not always gain by passing through the hands of the village musician.

IX. THE PRESENT-DAY REVIVAL OF THE FOLK-DANCE

TWENTY years ago the folk-dance had almost entirely disappeared, and the first definite effort made to reawaken it was that made by Mr D'Arcy Ferrers, who in 1886 revived the Morris

PRESENT REVIVAL OF FOLK-DANCE 159

dance in Bidford-on-Avon and round about that neighbourhood. This created great interest at the time, an interest which has since never wholly died out, though but for Mr D'Arcy Ferrers it is probable that the dances of that neighbourhood would have completely disappeared. At that time the traditional "side" had been disbanded, and Mr Ferrers reconstituted the dances from the little that remained in the memories of one or two old men.

He also taught them the tune of Arbeau's Morris dance which they used as "Morris Off," and to which they invented a dance which is quite in keeping with other traditional dances.

Later, in 1906, Lady Isabel Margesson interested herself in the dancers, and invited Mr Cecil Sharp and Mr H. C. MacIlwaine to Foxlydiat House, Redditch, where they took down the tunes and dances which were published in their first *Morris Book*. Later Miss Florence Warren went there to teach both these dances and others which had been collected in the meantime. The Bidford dances were also collected by Mr John Graham and published in *The Morris Dances of Shakspeare's Country*. In a recent edition of his *Morris Book*, Mr Cecil Sharp has omitted these Bidford dances, or retaken them from the Ilmington men, from whom they are believed to have originally been learnt.

But a more important revival took place in 1899, when Mr Percy Manning revived the Headington "Side," for in this case most of the dancers belonged to the traditional "Side." An entertainment was given at the Corn Exchange in Oxford, and the following interesting account of it appeared in the local papers:—"When the men danced in unison to the strains of a somewhat primitive fiddler quite a pretty effect was produced, whilst to the onlooker the spectacle was at once a convincing proof of its antiquity, so grotesque were the actions and gestures of the performers. The dance partakes somewhat of the nature of a hornpipe: there is a good deal of action in it, and it cannot be accused of too much sedateness or gravity. The troupe in each dance were accompanied by a fool, generally known as the Squire, who wore a diversified dress, consisting of a silk hat, decked with coloured ribbons, a white smock, and breeches, and one white and one brown stocking. He carried a stick with a bladder and a cow's tail at either end and frequently applied the stick to the back of the dancers."

The dances given at this revival were "The Blue-eyed Stranger," "Constant Billy," "Country Gardens," "Rigs o' Marlow," "How d'ye do, Sir?" "Bean-setting," "Haste to the Wedding," "Rodney," "Trunk Hose," and "Draw Back."

PRESENT REVIVAL OF FOLK-DANCE

It was during this revival at Headington that Mr Cecil Sharp first took down the tunes of the Morris dances which he afterwards gave to me in 1905. But this revised "side" of Morris men did not survive very long, and in 1905 or before had again given in and no longer danced down "The High" at Whitsuntide as in the old days.

But it was in 1905 that the real and, as I believe, permanent revival of the folk-dance first took place, and it happened in this way. For many years the Working Girls' Club, of which I am the honorary secretary, had devoted much time to learning national dances, and had already learnt the Scotch dances direct from two Scotchmen and the Irish dances from an Irish lady, so that we were quite ready to learn the English dances in the same way. Mr Cecil Sharp told me about the Headington Morris dancers, and gave me Mr William Kimber's address. I went to Headington and arranged for him and his cousin to come to London to teach the members of my Club. That first evening was a revelation to me, for I had never seen these London girls, with their natural aptitude for dancing in any form, quite so eager or so quick to learn. In two evenings they had mastered about four Morris dances, and were told by the instructors that they had got the dances quite perfectly.

ENGLISH FOLK-DANCE

The following account of that evening is taken from the first book of instructions by Mr Sharp and Mr MacIlwaine—

"The result of their coming far out-ran our fondest anticipations. The Morris, like the magic beanstalk, seemed to outwit the laws of nature: we saw it in the heart of London rise up from its long sleep before our very eyes. In connection with this affair, the mention of that well-beloved fable is appropriate and irresistible. The first dance that was set before these Londoners—upon this occasion which we enthusiasts make bold to call historic—was Bean-setting. It represents the setting of the seed in spring-time. Of course the music, its lilt and the steps that their forefathers had footed to it in the olden time, were as little known to these, the London born, as the tongue and ceremonial of old Peru. As little known, yet not strange at all; it was a summons never heard until now, yet instantly obeyed: because, though unfamiliar and unforeseen, it was of England, and came, even though it was centuries upon the way, to kinsfolk. Let the precisian explain it as he may, that is our way of accounting for an experience both fruitful and astounding. Within half-an-hour of the coming of these Morris men we saw the Bean-setting—its thumping and clashing of staves, its intricate

PRESENT REVIVAL OF FOLK-DANCE 163

figures and steps hitherto unknown—in full swing upon a London floor. And upon the delighted but somewhat dazed confession of the instructor, we saw it perfect in execution to the least particular. It was even so with the other dances; to see them shown was to see them learned."

That first evening's Morris dancing was the beginning of many happy hours of practice culminating in a demonstration of the dances and songs at a Christmas party held in the rooms of the Passmore Edwards' Settlement in 1905. The revival of the folk-dance, which was at once realised as genuine by many who were there, resulted in a more public performance in 1906, and from that date until the present day a series of Concerts has been given in London and within a radius of thirty miles around, and as far north as Yorkshire and south as Sussex. Besides this, the dancers were almost at once invited to teach the dances, and at the present time have taught in every county, and in villages, towns, schools, clubs, factories, and educational institutions from one end of England to the other. In 1909 the Board of Education sanctioned the dances being used as part of the course of physical exercises and organised play, but until after that sanction the members of the Espérance Club were the only teachers who had learnt their dances direct from the country dancers. The girls soon taught their men friends, and to-day as well as the girls we have several "Sides" of men who both teach and give displays of the dances. Since the visit of the first two Headington men, I have had over twenty dancers up to London, from Headington, Abingdon, Oddington, Yardley Gobion, Northampton, Lancashire, Warwickshire, Yorkshire, and other places, all of whom have contributed something to our direct knowledge of the dances still to be found in the country; and with Mr Clive Carey and others I have visited different centres of dancing with a view to bringing the dancers to London to teach, collecting all I could about old customs surviving around the dances and getting acquainted with the dancers. I have also sent some of our club members to the country with the same end in view. There is, therefore, at the present time a very strong link between the traditional dancers in the country and the young people in London who are busy practising and passing on the dances, and there is no longer any fear now that the dances will die out completely and be lost to the coming generations.

At first all we had to depend on when teaching the dance was the memory of our working girls who had first learnt the dances, and the manuscript of the music which Mr Sharp had taken down

PRESENT REVIVAL OF FOLK-DANCE 165

from the men who taught us. Thus it became necessary to make the record more permanent and to leave some guide to the dances with those whom we taught. Mr Sharp and Mr MacIlwaine, with the help of Miss Florence Warren, who danced again and again while the actual steps were being recorded, then published a book of tunes and instructions for the dances, and these have been followed by three more sets of the dances. Mr John Graham published two volumes very shortly after, and Mr Clive Carey, Mr Geoffrey Toye, and I followed with two volumes of tunes and instructions. We are all still engaged both in searching for dances, teaching them, and recording them for future use, and though probably the best and most characteristic dances are now duly recorded, still one is never sure where the work is really ended, and we shall always be glad to hear from any readers of fresh dances, which we shall be glad to investigate and, if genuine, record for future use.

In 1907 Mr Cecil Sharp and I disagreed over the constitution of a committee, and from that date have worked on entirely separate lines. I have kept very carefully to the traditional lines, making a great point of having those whom I send out to teach taught by country dancers without the intervention of professional dance instructors, so that to-day, after eight years' practice, I believe they are dancing as much like the original dancers as is possible.

After the recognition of the traditional dances by the Board of Education, Mr Sharp started a school of teachers at the London South-Western Polytechnic, and the teachers sent out from there have also taught in different parts of the country. As lately as 1911 these young ladies from the Polytechnic have formed the nucleus of the Folk-Dance Society, with Mr Sharp as Director, while the Espérance Club, as the Espérance Guild of Morris Dancers, also continues its work.

In 1910 I organised a vacation School at Littlehampton in Sussex, when sixty teachers from County Council Schools in different parts of the country met to learn the folk-dances, and later that year I transferred the School, with Miss Florence Warren and Mr Clive Carey as instructors in dance and song, at the request of the Governors of the Memorial Theatre at Stratford-on-Avon to that place, and about two hundred availed themselves of the opportunity of learning the songs and dances.

At this point, owing to Mr Sharp's criticism of our methods, it was decided to hold a conference to discuss points of difference with a view to making the work at Stratford-on-Avon both national and permanent. In view of this conference, I resigned my position as hon. secretary of the Folk-Dance School at Stratford-on-Avon. But no conference was held, and Mr Sharp was appointed Director of the School.

The School organised by the Espérance Guild was taken back to Littlehampton, and is held there every Easter.

A belated conference was held two years later, with no practical results.

It is hoped that in future some National Centre will be formed which will bring together all those interested in the collection and perpetuation of our English folk-dances, so that nothing of this National treasure be lost to future generations.

X. CONCLUSIONS

IN the foregoing pages we have seen how in primitive times dancing was inextricably interwoven with all religious ceremonial, even when that religion took the earlier form of magic and the dancing was part of a ceremonial to induce the growth of crops or the rising of the morning sun. We have seen, too, how later the more advanced teaching of the Greek and Christian religion was partly expressed and symbolised in dance and rhythmic gesture. We have seen these same dances as part of the popular festivities of the folk, gathered around May-day festivals, rude drama, wakes, lamb ales and rush-bearing, and attached still to the Church as part of the festivals of Christmas, Easter, and Whitsuntide.

And finally we have recorded the existence of these dances in villages and country towns in different parts of England at the present day, their recent revival, and the success which has attended their reintroduction to the present generation.

It is of the utmost importance that the nature of these dances should be clearly kept in mind by those who are responsible for their continuance. Until six years ago they were unrecorded in manuscript or print, they were only in the memory of the remaining Morris men, most of them old and quite unlettered, and there was no language in which to express the steps and evolutions but that invented by these peasant men. Neither could these cryptic sayings, such as "foot up," "half hands," "hey sides up," "gipsies," "half rounds," etc., etc., be interpreted except by a patient watching of the dancers on the few occasions when they could be got together to give a demonstration.

The following account of an old dancer will

CONCLUSIONS

give the atmosphere of the folk-dance and an idea of the way in which the Espérance Guild teachers have themselves learned the dances. I was speaking in a village at a "sing song" one evening when a man asked me if I had ever heard of certain dances and offered to give me the names of the then surviving dancers. I said "No," and he gave me the names.

I wrote to one of two brothers who still had the traditional dances and received the following reply:—

"Honourable and respected Miss,—

"I am the party what has got those dances, I shall be proud to show them to you, yours to command."

Eventually I went to see him, spent an afternoon in the bar parlour of a jolly little inn, and invited him and his brother up to London.

When they began to teach we found they had only one adjective between them and it was "perpendicular," and this word had to do duty many times during the evening. We were told we must "dance perpendicular to one another," "perpendicular to the music," and finally that we had got the dance "quite perpendicular"!

But I think we got hold of the dance, and that our boys and girls dance it much better than if they had been taught it by a professional dancer with technical terms and a settled technique; anyway, they love the dance, and it is always encored when we give it in public.

What, then, is the natural way for these ever-changing, ever-evolving dances to be passed on? I unhesitatingly say that they should be learnt in the first instance from the traditional dancer and passed on in the same way. The written instructions are only useful as a reminder of steps and evolutions, and should never be made an unalterable and fixed standard. For if folk-dancing has been evolving through all these countless generations, who shall fix the exact moment when evolution ceased and the steps and evolutions became fixed and unalterable? So far as I have seen traditional dancers, I have noticed that not only does every side in every village dance a little differently, but each man has his own way with the steps, and still further, the same man may dance differently every time he does the dance. I am behind no one in the desire that these dances shall be as accurately transcribed and as carefully taught as possible, and that the general character and atmosphere shall be preserved, but it is just because of this desire that I would have the dances as far as possible left to the interpretation of those who are unhampered by technical knowledge and unconfined by technical terms and academic restrictions.

CONCLUSIONS

In September 1912, I had up to town from Bampton two traditional dancers who imparted three dances, "The Rose Tree," "Glorisheers," and "The Flowers of Edinburgh," to a group of working boys and girls. About two months later these same boys and girls were teaching others the three dances. Looking on with great interest were six children, whose average age was eleven, all from elementary schools. These children had already learnt several of the Headington and Bidford dances, but had not seen the Bampton dances, the steps of which vary considerably from those of the two other places. In about an hour, as I thought it was rather dull for the children, I said, "Let me see if you can dance 'The Rose Tree' while the elder ones have a rest." The children were delighted with the suggestion, and to my surprise went through the dance almost perfectly as to both step and evolution. A few corrections and two more attempts, and the dance was quite correctly danced. This being a fact of which this is only one of many proofs, it is quite evident that a series of demonstrations by those who know the dance is all that is needed to pass it on to those interested enough to watch. There seems to be in these traditional dance movements something natural and inevitable, so that it is more easy to dance them correctly than to do them wrongly, and I think it is in this spirit that they should be taught. There is nothing strained and difficult, nothing artificial or exotic ; all is simple, dignified, vigorous, and joyful.

For this reason I have sometimes regretted that the folk-dance has become officially recognised as part of the school curriculum, and I regret too the necessity for books of instructions. I would rather the dances had remained in the memories of dancers and that the right atmosphere had been secured only by the verbal telling of folk tale and legend. But books seem to be a necessity to-day, and lest again we lose our national heritage of dance, perhaps it is well that some records have been made.

Another point that should be emphasised is that there should be as much interest as possible aroused in the collecting of these dances, and as much publicity as possible about the places where they are danced, the time of year when they can be seen, and the dancers who still hold the tradition. Probably the best dances are already in print; still, surprises of treasure still undiscovered may await us, and even if every known dance is already collected and published, nothing but good will come of this being done again and again by different people at different times. This will keep the traditional dances from becoming set and rigid, and will give a delightful air of spontaneity if at any folk festival, while all dance correctly, each dances a little differently from the others. Nothing is less to be desired than that any school or any individual should take possession of this national treasure; let all who are interested give of their best, whether as collectors, teachers, organisers, or writers, to the preservation of our National Folk-Dance.

BIBLIOGRAPHY

IN the space of the foregoing book it has been impossible to give more than a limited account of English Folk-Dance. Students are, therefore, referred to the following books—

"Dancing." Badminton Library. By Mrs Lily Grove. 1895.

"Educational Value of Dancing and Pantomime." By Dr Stanley Hall, Clarke University, Worcester, Mass.

"Illustrations of Shakespeare and of Ancient Manners." 2 vols. London, 1807. By Francis Douce. 1807.

"The Witch of Edmonton." By divers well estimed Poets, W. Rowley, T. Dekker, J. Ford, etc. 1658.

"History, Natural and Experimental, of Life and Death." Lord Bacon. 1638.

"Every Man out of His Humour." Ben Jonson. Act II. Sc. i. 1600.

"The Gypsies Metamorphosed." Gifford's Edition, reprinted by Lt.-Col. Cunningham. 1875. Vol. II.

"Women Pleased." J. Fletcher.

"Survey of London." By Strype. 1791.

"Orchesographie. Et Traicte en Forme de Dialogue." Par lequel toutes personnes peuvent facilement apprendre et pratiquer l'honneste exercice des dances." Par Thoinot-Arbeau (*i.e.* Jean Tabourot) demeurant - a - Langres. (22nd Nov., 1588.)

"The Vow Breaker, or Fair Maid of Clifton." William Sampson. 1636.

"Old Meg of Herefordshire for a Mayd Marian, and Hereford towne for a Morris-dance; or twelve Morris dancers in Herefordshire of 1200 years old." 1609.

"Survey of London," 1598, p. 72. Stowe.

"Antiquites Vulgares." Bourne. 1725.

"Natural History of Cornwall." Borlase. 1758.

"The British Bibliographer." Vol. IV.

"Popular Antiquities." Brand. The early and the later editions.

"English County Songs." Collected by Lucy E. Broadwood and J. A. Fuller Maitland. 1893.

"Mysterium und Mimus im Rigveda." By Leopold Von Schroeder. 1908.

"Old English Sports, Pastimes, and Customs." By Rev. P. H. Ditchfield. (Methuen, 1891.)

"Festivals, Games, and Amusements, Ancient and Modern." By Horatio Smith. (Colburn & Bentley, 1831.)

"A Picture of the Manners, Customs, Sports and Pastimes of the Inhabitants of England, from the arrival of the Saxons down to the Eighteenth Century." By J. Aspen. (J. Harris, St Paul's Churchyard, 1825.)

BIBLIOGRAPHY

"Book of Days." In 2 vols. Chambers. (W. & R. Chambers, London, 1863.)

"The Mediaeval Stage." In 2 vols. Chambers. 1903.

"Glig-Gamena, Angel-Deod, or The Sports and Pastimes of the People of England." By J. Strutt. (London, 1801.)

"Old Country Life." By S. Baring-Gould. (Methuen, 1890.)

"Shropshire Folk-Lore." Edited by C. S. Burne, from the collections of Georgina Jackson. (Trübner, 57 Ludgate Hill, 1883.)

"Rush-Bearing." An Account of Old Customs. By Alfred Burton. (Brook & Chrystal, Manchester, 1891.)

"Memoirs of Bartholomew Fair." By H. Morley. (Chatto & Windus, Piccadilly, 1880.)

"Popular Music of the Olden Times." 2 vols. By William Chappell, F.S.A. (London, 1855-59.)

"Lancashire Legends, Sports, etc." By J. Harland and T. Wilkinson. (J. Heywood, London, 1882.)

"Household Tales and Traditional Remains." By S. O. Addy. (D. Nutt, Strand, 1895.)

"British Goblins—Folk-Lore." By Wirt Sikes. (Sampson Low, Marston, 1880.)

"Manners, Customs, and Observances." By Leopold Wagner. (W. Heinemann, London, 1894.)

"Hone's Year Book." See vols. I., II., and IV. (T. Tegg, 73 Cheapside, 1832.)

"Brand's Popular Antiquities of Great Britain." By W. Carew Hazlitt. (J. Russel Smith, 36 Soho Square, 1870.)

"Traditions, Superstitions, and Folk-Lore." By C. Hardwick. (Simpkin, Marshall & Co., 1872.)

ENGLISH FOLK-DANCE

"The Gentleman's Magazine Library." Edited by G. L. Gomme. (See vol. on Manners and Customs, also vol. on Popular Superstitions.) (Elliot Stock, Paternoster Row, 1883.)

"The Study of Folk Song." By Countess Martinengo-Cesaresco. (G. Redway, York Street, 1886.)

"Folk-Lore." Mr Percy Manning's contributions to this Journal.

"Dictionary of Music and Musicians." 4 vols. Edited by Sir George Grove.

"The Pirate." Sir Walter Scott.

"Nine Days' Wonder performed on a Journey from London to Norwich." Kemp. 1600. (Arber, *English Garner*, II., 1903.)

"Shakespeare and his Times." 2 vols. Dr Nathan Drake. London, 1817.

"The Environs of London." 4 vols. Daniel Lyson. 1792-96.

"Shakespeare and Music." Edward W. Naylor, M.A., Mus. Bac. London, 1896.

"Lancashire and Cheshire Morris Dances." By John Graham.

"Shakespeare Morris Dances." By John Graham.

"The Morris Book." 3 vols. By Cecil Sharp and H. C. MacIlwaine.

"The Morris Book." 1 vol. By Cecil Sharp.

"Sword Dances of Northern England." By Cecil Sharp.

"Espérance Morris Book." 2 vols. Edited by Mary Neal.

"Dances of the Olden Time." A. Moffat and Frank Kidson.

INDEX

ADDISON's allusions to folk-song, 3, 80
Aird, James, his *Selection* (1788), 29

BALLAD, the narrative, 53
Ballad sheets and song garlands, 79
Ballad printers, 80
Baring-Gould, Rev. S., 43
Barrett, Dr W. A., 43, 44
"Basket of Oysters," 29, 30
Bewick, Thomas, 61, 84
Bibliography of folk-song and folk-music, 86
"Bonny Labouring Boy," 23
Boughton, Mr Rutland, 47
Broadwood, Rev. John, 41
Broadwood, Miss Lucy E., 43, 44, 75
Bunting, Edward, *Ancient Music of Ireland*, 33
Bussell, Mr F. W., 44

CANTE-FABLE, the, 15
Carols, 23, 74, 113
Chanty, the sea, 72
Chaplin's, Miss Nellie, revival of ancient dances, 157
Chappell, William, 41
Churchwardens' accounts, 112, 136
"Cock o' the North," 31, 32
Country dance, the, 152
Cox, Captain, his collection of ballads, 80

DANCE rhythm, 111
Dibdin, Charles, 61

Dickens, Charles, his *Nurse's Story*, 18
Dress, 136
Drinking songs, 62

ELIZABETHAN Morris dancing, 119
Engel, Carl, *Study of National Music*, 22
Espérance Working Girls' Club, revival of Morris dancing in, 161
Execution ballads, 66
Extra characters, 141

FERRERS', Mr D'Arcy, revival of Morris dancing, 158
Folk-dance, definition of, 97
Folk-music and folk-song, changes in, 25
    construction of, 19
    conventional passages in, 34
Folk-song, definition of, 10
    different classes of, 52
    difficulty of localizing, 39
    diffusion of, 37
    Indian, 12
    movement for collecting, 40
    Society, its origin and members, 45
    suggested origin of, 11
    the noting of, 47
Fool, the, 142
Fraser, Mrs Kennedy, 74
French songs, their popularity in England, 6
Furry dance, 150

GARDINER, Mr H. Balfour, 47
Gilchrist, Miss A. G., 22, 46

M 177

Goosey dancing, 151
Grainger, Mr Percy, 46
"Greensleeves," 5, 27, 28
Grove's *Dictionary of Music and Musicians*, 22

HEBRIDES, songs of the, 74
Highwayman songs, 64
Hobby horse, the, 143
Hone's, William, *Ancient Mysteries*, 76
Humorous songs, 62
Hunting and sporting songs, 70

JACOBS', Mr, *English Fairy Tales*, 15
"Joan's Placket is torn," 32

LABOUR, songs of, 71
Lancashire Morris dance, words of, 135
Laneham's "Letter," 80
Legge, Mr Robin H., 74
Love songs, 57

MANNING'S, Mr Percy, revival of Morris dancing, 160
Mason, Miss A. H., 43
Mayor of the Morris, 142
Modern dancers' dress, 139
Modes, the ecclesiastical, 19
Moore, Thomas, *Irish Melodies*, 29
Morris dances, list of, 128
Morris dances, where found, 130
Morris dancing, books on, 125
Morris dancing in later times, 122
"Morris," derivation of word, 99
Mummers' play, 99
Musical instruments, 132
Mysterium und Mimus im Rigveda, 146
Mystic songs, 57

"ONE Moonlight Night," 22

Orange, the story of, 17

"PADDY the Weaver," 29
Pastoral songs, 60
Percy's, Bishop, *Reliques of Antient Poetry*, 47
Pictures of Morris dancers, 119
Playford's *Dancing Master*, 153
Poaching songs, 64
Present-day teaching, 170
Pressgang songs, 69
Primitive religious customs, 102, 144
Printers of ballads and garlands, 80

RHYTHMS, mixed, 49

"SAILOR loved a Farmer's Daughter, A," 33
Salii, the, 101
Sea chanties, 72
Sea songs, 67
"Shamrock Shore," 24
Sharp, Mr Cecil J., 15, 47, 75
Sharp's, Mr Cecil, revival of Morris dancing, 159
Sheppard, Rev. H. F., 44
Singing games, 77
Soldier songs, 66
Spectator quoted, 3, 80
Stanton, Mrs, 33
Stokoe, Mr John, 42
Stratford-on-Avon, 166
Sword dance, 145

TOLMIE, Miss, 74
Treasurer, the, 144
Tunes, 130

VACATION School at Littlehampton, 166

WALTON'S *Compleat Angler*, 79
Williams, Dr Vaughan, 47

Lightning Source UK Ltd.
Milton Keynes UK
UKHW041238161119
353476UK00015B/5/P